How to Be the Parent Your Teenager Needs You to Be

Without all of the Fighting, Frustration, or Fear of Doing it Wrong

By
Jim White
Family Enrichment Coach

FAMILY ENRICHMENT

ACADEMY

© 2022 Jim White

All Rights Reserved.

No portion of this book may be reproduced, stored in a retrieval system, or transmitted in any form or by any means – electronic, mechanical, photocopy, recording, scanning, or other – except for brief quotations in critical reviews or articles, with the prior written permission of the author.

This book is dedicated to the healing power of love and the impact it can have on all of our families.

Table of Contents

vi

Introduction:

I am going to show you how to be the parent your teenager needs you to be without the fighting, frustration, or fear of doing it wrong. Now, I am guessing for a lot of you this is not the first time you have gone looking for help on how to be a better parent. And since you are here, my guess is you still aren't sure that you have found what you are looking for. There is so much information and advice out there that it can be overwhelming. The first thing I want you to know is that it's okay to be uncertain.

If you have been concerned or afraid that you just don't have what it takes to be the parent your child needs you to be, I want to put those fears to rest. You definitely have what it takes. It is in there, and all you need is the right person to help you find what is going to work best for your family.

As parents we are all fighting against a lot of outside influences: social media, YouTube, TikTok, Netflix, video games, and of course peer pressure. Our children—and to be honest, all of us—are being bombarded with conflicting messages that cause us to question everything. How late is too late for my teenager to stay up? Would they be better off at a different school? What is the best way to discipline? There are a million questions.

I am here to assure you that hope is not lost. It is possible to be exactly the parent your child needs you to be. It is possible to raise happy, well-adjusted children who will go out into the world and make a difference.

Also, I would like to say thank you. I am saying thank you now because I am pretty sure that your teenager is not going to see you reading this book and feel compelled to run up to you, give you a hug, and say thanks for making the commitment to being a better parent. So on behalf of your teenager, the teachers at their school, their future employers, their future roommates and families—thank you for not settling for just getting by. Thank you for your commitment to being better than you were yesterday and listening to the call for love.

The goal for this book and the accompanying 28-Day Parenting Boot Camp is to reveal the key to transforming your relationship with your teenager while providing a framework for putting these strategies into practice. Here is a sneak preview: Love is always the answer. More on this to come.

> "Once you choose hope, anything is possible."
> —Christopher Reeve

Part 1: My Story

My family story starts in high school. I made what turned out to be an awesome decision in the summer before my sophomore year. I was given the opportunity to choose between two high schools. I could go to the school where all of my friends would be going or I could go to a brand-new high school where I would have the opportunity to play varsity football my sophomore year. I chose the new school and football over staying with my friends. Little did I know that this decision would lead me to a beautiful young woman who would eventually become my wife. Looking back, it seems like God may have had my back.

Anne and I were married in 1982, and a few years after our marriage we had our first child. Like all new parents I wanted to do a good job, but to be honest I wasn't really sure what that meant. On one level, I knew that I was responsible for the physical care of my son. That meant not dropping him or losing him in the store. But on a deeper level I wanted him to be "successful," to be happy, to be a good person.

A list of things I wanted for him began to form in my mind:

- I wanted my son to be respectful to other adults and have a pleasant personality.
- I wanted my son to be the one who recognized that there was a new kid in school and be welcoming in the lunchroom.
- I wanted my son to be the one who would stop his buddies from speaking disrespectfully about girls at school.
- I wanted my son to have the self-confidence to say no when he was offered drugs at a party.
- I wanted my son to find his purpose in life and throw himself into something he was passionate about.

To be honest, I was not even sure if I could accomplish that last point for myself, so how was I supposed to teach my child? But here's the thing about becoming a parent: There is no turning back.

So over the next 15 years, I was really careful on the care-taking stuff, and when it came to teaching my son how to be a "good" person, I did what seemed to make sense. I taught him to say please and thank you, we worked on sharing with and being kind to others, and I helped with homework. You get the idea.

By the way, we also had five more children over those 15 years.

Around the time our sixth child was born, my life took an unexpected turn. It started with an invitation to join a Toastmasters group. Toastmasters International is an organization that promotes communication skills. The primary benefit of joining this club is the opportunity to give short speeches on a regular basis to other members, who then respond with constructive criticism and feedback.

In order to focus on delivery techniques and getting over any stage fright, we were encouraged to talk about topics we were comfortable with. Being a father of six children, I found myself talking about dad stuff. In fact, I found myself focusing on the idea of teaching my children how to be "good" and "successful" people.

Aha moment:

My approach to giving a speech at Toastmasters was to write the talk out word for word. I had never taken the time to write before. As you can imagine, life in our family was very busy. Between school functions, sports, homework, earning a living, and the everyday tasks needed to manage a home with six children, I had never taken the time to stop and reflect, let alone write down my thoughts or actually read any of the self-improvement books I had bought.

I started going to lunch by myself. I would take my computer and a book on parenting or personal development. I would read for 15 or 20 minutes and then I would write. The speech writing became a form of journaling, and I quickly became very attached to the process. After a couple of years of writing speeches, I thought to myself, "You know, I have enough here for a book." But I quickly realized that I needed a way to connect these lessons.

As I sat there at lunch with my computer in front of me, I thought the first thing I needed to do was clarify the goal. What is it I am trying to accomplish through these stories and lessons? So I wrote this definition of a *successful family*:

> **A *successful family* is one whose members speak with respect, honor difference, provide**

a nurturing environment, empower each other, and truly enjoy being together.

This family has a knack for really enjoying and appreciating the good times, while at the same time, they can effectively deal with any difficult issues that come their way. There is a sense of peace, joy, warmth, and love within their home.

Think of this definition as the north star. This is what we aspire to in our families.

As I read what I had written that day, the obvious question was: If this was the ultimate goal for my family, how do we get there?

As I took a bite of my sandwich and read over this definition of a "successful" family, I had one of those moments of clarity. An *aha* moment.

What I realized about my family and all of the other families I had been around is that the "great" moments— the moments that lived up to this definition—were always grounded in love. And the moments that were not so great— the moments that looked nothing like this definition—were always grounded in fear.

I realized at that moment that the secret to creating a *successful family* was to be very **INTENTIONAL** about choosing love over fear regardless of the circumstance.

The key point here is not recognizing the power that love can have in our families. Most of us can appreciate this. The *aha* moment was realizing that we have the power to choose how we engage within our families. The secret is to be intentional about choosing love regardless of the circumstance, even in the heat of the moment.

4

So when it comes to parenting your teenager, think of it this way: All of us have two separate thought systems that live inside of us—a love-based thought system and a fear-based thought system.

With every circumstance or situation, we have the power to choose how we will respond. In most cases, however, we respond out of habit or past conditioning. But we do have the power to choose our response whether we exercise it or not.

Controlling vs. empowering

When it comes to parenting your teenager, these two thought systems produce fundamentally different approaches. We either engage with the goal of *controlling* or we engage with the intention of *empowering*.

When the goal is *control*, we make demands and use punishment and reward. Furthermore and most important: I realized that our need to control is fear based.

When the intention is to *empower*, we teach, coach, and connect. Empowerment is love based.

Another way of saying this is that when we are grounded in fear, our natural response as a parent is to try to control the circumstances. Whereas when we are grounded in love, our natural response is to empower our teenager to be their absolute best.

If the goal is to move your family toward the definition of a *successful family* I have offered, then it is important for you to continually develop your ability to intentionally choose love, regardless of the circumstance, so that you will naturally be a source of empowerment regardless of the circumstance—regardless of how life is putting the squeeze on you.

This idea is the foundation for the work we do at The Family Enrichment Academy. Everything we do is designed to move families along their journey toward **INTENTIONALLY** choosing love. Love is always the answer.

This is our big idea. If this speaks to you, you are in the right place, in the right community. If it doesn't, then I would recommend that you continue to search for teachings that speak to you. One of the keys to empowerment is learning to listen to and trust your intuition and inner wisdom.

Here is a parenting example of what it means to be intentional in choosing love-based empowerment over fear-based control:

My daughter Rachel was approaching her 16th birthday, and as we all know this usually is the time in a young person's life when they learn to drive. As with all of her brothers and sisters, I was the designated driving instructor within the family. Teaching a child to drive starkly brings out the contrast between the parental choice between control and empowerment. By definition, in order for Rachel to learn to drive, I had to turn control of the car over to her. If you have taught anyone to drive, you can appreciate how uncomfortable it feels to sit in the passenger seat as you pull out onto the street for the first time. In effect, I was forced to choose empowerment because I didn't have control of the car.

I should note that I taught all of our six children how to drive, and my struggle between control and empowerment was the same with all of them. I am telling Rachel's story because of the twist we experienced at the end.

As Rachel and I are starting down our neighborhood street, the conflict within my head starts. On one hand, I want to start barking orders: *You are going too fast! ... You are too close to the mailboxes! You need to start slowing down sooner when you are coming up to a stop sign!* On the other hand, I know that if I say these things from a place of frustration, anger, or fear for my life, they will only make her feel more anxious and overwhelmed. You may be thinking that these instructions were important information that she needed to be aware of in order to be a good driver. True. But there is a big difference between engaging in this situation from a need to control and an intention to empower.

Here is how it might go if I am coming from a need to control:

As we start down the street I say with a little frustration: *Rachel you are way too close to these mailboxes on the right. You have got to pay more attention to your surroundings.*

Rachel feeling anxious and attacked: *I am trying.*

As we continue down the road, I say again, with ager in my voice: Come on, Rachel, you are still way too far to the right!

Rachel starts getting defensive: *Well, if you would stop yelling at me I could concentrate on what I am doing.*

I know for some of you this sounds very familiar. So here is the alternative. Here is how it could go if I am very intentional about choosing love-based empowerment:

Before we even get in the car, I remind myself that learning to drive is a huge deal to Rachel. She is going to be full of emotions. She will be excited while at the same time being

7

nervous, worried, and afraid. I strive to stay aware of how she is doing emotionally and be compassionate. Can you see how I am being intentional about my mindset?

Next, before she puts the car into gear, I set the stage by saying: *I know learning to drive is very exciting, but I also know that it can be a scary experience* (with a little smile to lighten the mood) *for both of us. I am going to try really hard to stay compassionate and patient, and I would like for you to try really hard to stay calm and open to my coaching. Does that sound fair?*

Rachel: *Yeah, I will try.*

Then I say (again we haven't left the driveway yet): *One of the things I am going to be doing is giving you feedback on where you are on the road. Too far right or too far left. It won't take long for you to get a feel for it, but in the beginning when I say "you are drifting right or drifting left," notice where you are on the road, what it looks like to you, and then make a correction. Sound good?*

Rachel: *Okay.*

Now as we are driving down the street and the upcoming mailbox is in grave danger, I say with compassion and support: *You are drifting right.*

Rachel makes the correction and the mailbox is spared.

To be honest, in that moment, when we are heading right for a mailbox, it is really hard to resist the urge to control the circumstance. And in fact, sometimes it is necessary to reach over and turn the steering wheel. But when you zoom out and focus on the end goal, which in this case is to give Rachel the skills and more importantly the judgment necessary to drive a car safely, empowerment is clearly more effective than control. She has to be able to do this on her own without me in the passenger seat within reach of the steering wheel.

Now here is the twist that we experienced with Rachel. When she went for her driver's test, she drifted right and momentarily her right wheels were off the road, which is an automatic fail. And because of a newly enacted change in our state's laws, she could not retake the driving test for six months. As you can imagine, when she pulled back up with the driving instructor, she was devastated. Six months is an eternity to a 16-year-old who wants her driver's license.

Life was putting the squeeze on us and our daughter. We could react out of disappointment, frustration, and anger. Or we could respond with compassion and forgiveness. This was an opportunity to choose between control and empowerment. Between fear and love. I am happy to report that we chose empowerment and love. We coached her through the process of making an action plan for developing her driving skills. When one of her friends would get their license and she was reliving her disappointment and frustration over failing, we would listen with compassion. When she was discouraged, we would offer hope by reminding her of her talents and all that she had accomplished in her life. Six months later, she passed her second test without any issues. Interestingly, a few years later, Rachel told us that when she looks back on this series of events she has to admit that she wasn't really ready to drive on her own the first time she took the test. The additional practice was a good thing. One of my wife's favorite sayings is that "things always happen for a reason."

The continuum

When I wrote my definition of a *successful family*, the intention was to create an ideal image. A target for all families to aspire to. My family has had times when we have experienced peace, joy, warmth, and love. Times where someone would look at us and say: *There goes a family that meets the definition of a successful family.* But we have also had times when we didn't. There have been times when our house was full of disappointment, frustration, and anger. We have not been kind to each other. The environment within our home was destructive.

I like to think of it all as a continuum. Each minute of the day, you are either experiencing the joy and peace of love or you are experiencing the difficulties that arise from fear. Think about the last 24 hours. How many of the last 1440 minutes were joyful and how many were not. Was it 50-50? Or was it a better day...maybe 75% joyful? Maybe it was a difficult day and you would say only 10% joyful. The purpose of this work is to move you along this continuum. To support the growth of your family and your own personal growth so that you experience more and more peace, joy, warmth, and love each day.

As I have gone through my life as a husband, father, and now grandfather, the part of the *successful family* definition that has had the biggest impact on my family is this: *"while at the same time, they have the ability to effectively deal with any difficult issues that come their way."* What I am describing here is the ability to recover. It is kind of like when the heart doctor has a patient do a stress test. Part of the test is an evaluation of the patient's heart rate and breathing while running or walking fast—while under stress.

But equally important is the patient's ability to recover and return to a resting heart and breathing rate.

There is no way around this. You and your family are going to experience "difficult issues." My family certainly has. At the writing of this book, my wife and I have been married for nearly 40 years. We have had our share of sunny days, but we have also had a lot of cloudy days. During our 40 years, we have also had three hurricanes within our marriage. These were periods when divorce was discussed. We have grieved the loss of my wife's parents and my father. We have struggled with our finances. With regards to our children and parenting, we have experienced everything from a bad grade on a test to being cut from a team to sitting in a courtroom while our son was being tried for reckless driving to struggles with drugs and alcohol.

The point is that one of the key factors that determines the success of your family is your ability to recover from the inevitable "bad luck" that will come your way.

Here is an analogy I came across a few years ago that will provide some additional context for the idea of being intentional and the importance of your mindset. I often use this analogy in my talks and workshops.

Orange analogy (modeled after Dr. Wayne Dyer's presentation)

As I hold an orange up, I will say to the audience:

"I have in my hand an orange. The orange is a wonderful piece of fruit. So let me ask you a question. If I squeeze this orange, what will come out?" I also explain to them that this analogy is not a riddle; these questions are not intended to be trick questions.

At this point, someone will usually respond with the obvious answer: "Orange juice."

To which I will respond, "Is there any way I can squeeze this orange and get apple juice? Maybe if I squeeze it real hard from the bottom up? Or if I squeeze it from right to left, could I ever get grape juice?"

This is the point where I can see a lot of puzzled faces in the audience. I can tell they are wondering where this is going as they shake their heads.

Then I will ask one more question: "Why is that? Why do you get orange juice when you squeeze an orange?" I remind them again that this is not a trick question.

After a few moments, someone will typically say something like, "Because it's an orange." To which I respond, "Exactly. When you squeeze an orange, orange juice comes out because that is what is inside of the orange...right?"

Next, I reveal the point of the analogy by saying, "Now let's extend this analogy to you. Let's say life puts the squeeze on you. That is to say, someone said something that offends you or someone does something you don't like or you are dealt a difficult circumstance. What comes out of you? Frustration...anger disappointment...hatred? Now, you are quick to say that the reason the frustration, anger, disappointment, and hatred are coming out is because of what that person said, or what they did, or because of what happened to you. But the truth of the matter is that you are just like the orange.

What comes out is what is on the inside.

But the good news is that unlike the orange, if you don't like what is coming out of you, you can change it. You have the power to choose your thought system.

I don't know about you, but when I first heard this I had another one of those *aha* moments. It became super clear that personal development or family development was an *inside out process*. If I want to change how I am acting and what I am experiencing—or as a parent if I want to change how my children are acting or what they are experiencing— the focus needs to be on what is going on inside of myself or inside of my children.

This analogy created a visual image for me. The image of life putting the squeeze on me and the realization that my actions were a reflection of my inner world. What are the principles, values, and beliefs that shape how they see and respond to the world? For me, this is very empowering. Instead of being the victim of my circumstances or -instead of my children being the victim of their circumstances, we have a choice.

The title of this book is **How to BE the Parent Your Teenager Needs You to BE**. I'm putting emphasis here on this idea of being. Parents are always asking me what they should do in a particular situation. While this is a valid question, it is not the first question. Before you can determine the best course of action, you must first ask yourself if you are viewing the circumstance from a loving or from a fearful perspective. In other words, what is going on inside you? My life experience has taught me that fundamentally these are the only two choices. You are either grounded in love or you are grounded in fear. In the following chapters, we will explore this idea in great depth. For now I invite you to

13

be open to the possibility that transforming your family is an *inside out process*.

I heard Dr. Wayne Dyer tell a valuable follow-up story to the orange analogy:

A saint or holy person was speaking with a crowd of people and was asked the following: You are so loving and kind…, and your presence brings peace to everyone you are around and you seem to have so much patience and compassion. What is the secret to being like this? Do you have knowledge of a special kind of love?

The saint responded, No, you and I both have the same love inside of us. There's nothing special about me. The difference between you and me is that I don't have anything else inside of me but love."

So what happened next? I finished writing the book and had it published in 2004 under the title *Because I Said So - The 12 Great Character Lessons of Our Youth*.

It was about this time that I discovered the profession of life coaching and attended the iPEC coaching program. I had become a self-improvement, personal development, spiritual development, and—even more importantly—a family enrichment geek.

So today I find myself being called to share what I have learned over the last 40 years as a husband, father, and now grandfather. In order to fulfill this calling, I have started an educational organization called The Family Enrichment Academy. Our mission is to empower parents to intentionally choose love over fear regardless of the circumstance or how life is putting the squeeze on them. To create love-based communities one *successful family* at a time.

Family update: My oldest son, Jake, is married with three children. Brittany, our second, is married with six children. Brianne, our third oldest, is married with three children. Jimmy, our fourth, was married this year. Rachel, our fifth, is happily single, and Isabella, our youngest, is a sophomore in college.

A hero's two journeys

Parenting has been a personal development program for me.

Think back to when your teenager was younger and you would watch all of those great Disney movies. What makes these movies so great is the storytelling structure of "a hero's two journeys." Whether your favorite was *The Lion King*, *Finding Nemo*, or *Toy Story*, all of these follow this simple storytelling process, with the hero undertaking a mission or a journey of some kind. Simba in *The Lion King* has run away; Marlin, Nemo's dad, is trying to find his son; and Woody feels obligated to bring Buzz Lightyear back. These are the outside journeys. But what makes these movies so compelling is the inside journey each of these heroes are on. As each of them strive to accomplish the outside goal, they find themselves being transformed on the inside. They are becoming not just different but a better person. Simba discovers that you should learn from your past and not run away from it. Marlin overcomes his fear and limiting beliefs about Nemo. Woody realizes that being Andy's favorite toy is not what makes him special, it is doing the right thing.

I invite you to consider the possibility that you are the hero in your family story. The outside mission is to raise your children to be "successful." You want them to be happy. To find joy and purpose in what they do and in their relationships as adults. But as I said earlier, how can you teach them or lead them to this type of success if you aren't sure how to accomplish it for yourself? As the hero in this story, you are also on an internal journey of transformation. As a parent, you are in a position to experience tremendous personal growth. Let's look back to the definition of a *successful family* I offered earlier, but this time with it shifted to the idea of a *successful person*":

A *successful person* is one who speaks with respect, honors difference, provides a nurturing environment, empowers others. and is a joy to be around.

They have a knack for really enjoying and appreciating the good times, while at the same time, they have the ability to effectively deal with any difficult issues that come their way.

They inspire a sense of peace, joy, warmth, and love wherever they go.

The most effective way to teach or influence your children is to lead by example. In fact, you are doing this whether you know it or not. Your children are always watching and listening to you. You are their hero. One of the greatest gifts you can give your child is to be very intentional and transparent about your journey to be a better person.

This is why the title of this book is *How to BE the Parent Your Teenager Needs You to BE.*

Part 2: Three Key Insights

Before we explore the specific strategies and techniques for shifting your mindset, building connection, and empowering your teenager, there are three insights I would like to share. These insights are intended to deepen your resolve and answer a few lingering questions I typically hear from the families I work with.

First, you may be questioning the fundamental premise that love is always the answer.

It is also common for parents to question how a shift in mindset is really going to make that much of a difference.

Finally, I often hear the comment that it doesn't really matter if I try these ideas, my teenager never listens to me anyway.

Let's look at each of the concerns.

Insight # 1—Choosing love and the shift to empowerment

Let's start by taking a look at the definition of *empowerment* from the Oxford Dictionary:

17

The process of becoming stronger and more confident, especially in controlling one's life.

Or (from Wikipedia):

It encourages **people to gain the skills and knowledge that will allow them to overcome obstacles in life or work environment and ultimately**, help them develop within themselves or in the society.

These definitions at first glance seem to describe the goal of parenting: giving your children the ability to make their way through life. But there is a second, equally as important part to our goal as parents.

Simply put: We want our children to experience peace, joy, and happiness. I have heard my wife say, "You are only as happy as your least happy child."

Think about all of the things that you want for your child:

- To get good grades
- To get the lead in the school play
- To win the starting position on the soccer team
- To get into a good college
- To find some good friends
- To stay out of trouble
- To learn to manage their money

Here is a question I want you to ask yourself: Why do you want these things for your child?

Stop for a minute and really think about this.

Ultimately, we want all of these things for our children because we believe that these successes will create a sense of peace, joy, and happiness for them.

This is a good time to consider again the idea of a hero's two journeys. While these outside goals and accomplishments are important, they are not the whole story. Your teenager is also going through an internal transformation. As parents, we have a role to play in this second journey as well. We have the opportunity to empower them along their journey of personal growth and development.

This is why the Insight #1 is:

Choosing love and the shift to empowerment

The true source of peace, joy, and happiness lies within us and within our child. So while we are empowering them to accomplish their outside goals or overcome obstacles, we are also empowering them toward an inner life of peace, joy, and happiness.

Ask yourself: How would you approach each goal or circumstance your teenager faces differently if their personal growth and development was the first priority and the outside goal was the second priority?

Here is a story that illustrates these both outside and inside opportunities for empowerment:

Our oldest son Jake had been a good student throughout elementary school and junior high school. His freshman year of high school was the same, mostly A's and a B here and there. In his sophomore year there were a few more B's but nothing overly concerning for my wife and me. His junior year was a lot tougher. This was the first time we had experienced this, but the junior year of high school proved to be a challenge for all of our children. Looking back now, I think it is a combination of more difficult coursework, the newfound independence of getting their driver's license, and a growing interest in activities other than school. Consequently, Jake's grades continued to slip.

Junior year is also a big year in terms of preparing to apply for college. Jake's dream since he was old enough to understand the idea of going to college was to attend Indiana University in Bloomington. So he took the SAT and started investigating the requirements to be accepted into his dream school, IU. This is when the conflict emerged between Jake and his mother and me. As parents, it was clear to us that while Jake had met the requirements for grade point average and SAT score, he was certainly not putting forth his best effort as a student. At this point, we sat him down and explained that while he may be qualified to get into Indiana University, we weren't interested in sending him there and paying for it if he wasn't going to give it his best effort. As you could have predicted, our words fell on deaf ears. Over the second semester of his junior year, we had this same conversation multiple times, but there was no change in his efforts. He had figured out what he needed to do to get by, and at the time this was good enough for him.

Jake's senior year started with the same "do enough to get by" approach to his studies.

An additional note: I should point out that a smart teenager can be really good at doing just enough to get by. Their intelligence allows them to identify the line they shouldn't cross as well as the gray areas on both sides of the line. They also have this uncanny ability to know exactly how much effort they need to make to stay in the good graces of their parents or teachers. If they need a B in a class, and in order to get a B they need to get an 80% on the final, they will get an 80.5%.

Back to Jake's story: At this point, my wife and I were starting to discuss the reality of taking a stand on our earlier statements concerning Jake's efforts and our willingness to pay for his college. Oblivious to the economics, Jake sent off his application for admission to Indiana University at the start of his senior year.

About halfway through the first semester of his senior year, a letter arrived from IU. Jake excitedly opened the letter expecting confirmation of his acceptance into the university. One short sentence communicated a great life lesson for him. The letter thanked him for his application but said he was being deferred. As you can imagine, this was certainly one of those moments where life was putting the squeeze on our son. Mixed in with a lot of emotions were a lot of questions.

Jake asked:

What does it mean to be deferred? How can this happen when my grade point average and test scores are so high?

I still get to go next year...right?

I have to admit this was also one of those moments where life was putting the squeeze on me. I remember experiencing a mix of frustration, disappointment, and fear. I was frustrated that Jake hadn't listened to me and my wife over the last year. I was disappointed in my effectiveness as a father. And I was afraid about how this was going to affect my son and his life. This was also one of those moments where I remember noticing myself being caught up in a fearful perspective. As we stood there in my home office, Jake's hands shaking as he held the letter from IU, I realized that I had a choice to make. I could continue to view this circumstance from a fearful perspective and let my frustration, disappointment, and fear guide my actions or I could reframe the situation from a loving perspective. As I was getting ready to launch into the "I told you so" lecture, I stopped. I shifted perspective and saw that what my son needed at this moment was to know he was in a safe, loving environment. Before we could begin to think about a plan of action, he would need to process all of the negative emotions and energy.

My objective quickly shifted from expressing my disappointment to just being there with Jake. This was a time to be compassionate and forgiving. To be honest, I didn't say very much. My focus was on staying grounded in a loving mind set. The interesting thing about compassion and forgiveness is that they can be communicated without words. After a few minutes went by, I could tell he was starting to regain his composure. He was not ready to start exploring his options, but I could tell he felt the loving presence of his parents.

So the next day, Jake came to us and asked the obvious question: What does it mean to be deferred? This was our signal that it was time to shift into love-centered empowerment mode. Jake's outside objective was to be able to attend Indiana University the following fall. While his inside transformation was not part of Jake's stated goals, we (my wife and I) recognized this circumstance as an opportunity for his character development. Interestingly, this kind of growth can only be gained through personal experience. It is kind of like learning to ride a bike. You can read all of the books, watch all of the videos, and pass all of the tests on how to ride a bike, but the only way to actually learn how to ride a bike is to get on it and try to ride. This was a problem that Jake needed to solve himself. Just like when he learned how to ride a bike, I would run alongside him to help him regain his balance if he started to fall, but in the end it was up to him.

The first order of business was a call to the admissions office. Jake learned that while his overall grade point average was above the minimum requirement, the admissions advisor was concerned with his declining grades. It was still possible for Jake to be accepted into IU, but in order to be admitted he would have to show improvement in his first semester senior year. The challenge was that he was already half of the way through this semester and had been working at his "do enough to get by" pace. Looking from the perspective of loving empowerment, my role was not to design a study plan and make sure it was followed. Instead, first, my role was to communicate my belief that he could overcome this obstacle if he put his mind to it. He had the ability, but it was going to be up to him to do the work. Secondly, my role was to provide coaching if he ever got stuck. The challenge with coaching is to resist providing the answers. The coach's role is to ask questions that move the person being coached, in this case Jake, toward finding their own answers. We will be exploring coaching strategies in greater depth in the following chapters, but the primary tools are open-ended questions.

For example: When we learned that Jake would need to show improvement in his grades before he would be admitted into Indiana University, I reminded him that he had gotten good grades before, so it was possible. Then I asked, "What do you want to do?" As a parent, sometimes the hard part of asking questions like this is the fear of what answer might be given. But these questions offer a growth opportunity for us to reframe the situation from a loving perspective. At this moment it is not about what we want, it is about helping your child discover what they want and to be present with our child in support of both their outer goal as well as their inner journey.

Jake laid out a plan for improving his grades and, more importantly, he made a commitment to give it his best effort. I am happy to report that he did accomplish the outer goal of being admitted to IU, but he also experienced an inner transformation. He had learned the value of making a commitment and giving his best effort. It is this inner growth that will continue to serve him throughout his life.

The wings of transformation grow out of patience and struggle.

Insight #2—You have the power to choose your perspective…and a change in perspective changes everything.

Take a look at this image. Can you see the head of a rabbit? Now, can you shift your perspective and see the duck? You may find that the more you look at this image, the easier it becomes to shift between the rabbit and duck. In effect, you can choose which image you wish to see. This is a demonstration of your power to choose your perspective.

Now, with this exercise, most people find the process of shifting their perspective relatively easy. But when life puts the squeeze on us...squeezing us like that orange...it can be more challenging. I would assert that we still have the power to choose, but we often are either so invested in one particular view that we hold on to it and don't even look for other perspectives or we are looking but just can't see an alternative perspective. In either case we are stuck.

Consider these points:

Could it be possible for two people to look at this image and be in disagreement as to what is pictured? One would insist that this is a picture of a rabbit, while the other would insist that it is a duck. Who is "right" and who is "wrong"? Interestingly, the image has not changed. It is just the perspective of the individuals that creates the disagreement.

Let's extend this thought to a life circumstance. For example: On your way home from work you find yourself in a traffic jam. Could it be possible for two people to view this circumstance from different perspectives?

Here is a very important point: Each individual's experience and subsequent actions are caused by their perspective, NOT by the circumstance—in this case, the traffic jam. Have you ever heard the idea that your inner world creates your outer world? One of our two travelers could see the traffic jam as a huge inconvenience. Consequently, they are experiencing frustration and anger about the delay. Their actions could include pounding the steering wheel and yelling at the other drivers. Our other traveler could see the traffic jam offering a much needed time to relax. Consequently, they are experiencing a sense of relief.

Their actions could include closing their eyes and taking deep breaths. Again, each individual's experience and subsequent actions are the result of their perspective on the circumstance rather than the circumstance itself.

You may be saying to yourself, "So what? It is a picture of a rabbit and a duck." But I would invite you to consider the possibility that your ability to exercise your power to choose how you see the world is the key to transforming your family. Furthermore, whether intentional or not, you are always making choices and those choices have a huge impact on your life experience and the lives of the people around you, including your teenager.

Over your lifetime I am sure you have heard many statements or pieces of advice that point to the importance of perspective. Do any of these sound familiar?:

- Your attitude controls your altitude.
- The right perspective makes the impossible possible.
- If you change the way you look at things, the things you look at change.
- It is not what you look at that matters, it is what you see.
- Happiness is found when you stop comparing yourself to others.
- The grass is always greener on the other side.

Here is an example of how a shift in perspective can change everything. One day, our 15-year-old daughter Bri came home from school completely frustrated about the "horrible" teacher she had for biology. Of course, it is nearly impossible for a teenager to get through high school without having at least one bad teacher (or one they believe to be "bad"). On one hand, I was happy about her frustration because it was a sign that she was invested in her education or at least in getting a good grade in this class. On the other hand, it was difficult as a parent to accept that this other person was causing such pain for my daughter. The obvious question was "What do you mean when you say they are a horrible teacher?" As my wife and I listened to Bri's long list of examples, it was hard not to shift into fix-it mode. Also, I felt myself being pulled into her frustration. This was the point when I realized that life was putting the squeeze on me. I could either continue to sink into her frustration—worried about her grades, worried about her ability to handle this situation and the impact this was going to have on her self esteem, worried about failing her as a father. Or I could see the potential in her and see this as an opportunity for my daughter's personal development—and an opportunity for my development as a parent.

Put yourself in this situation. Imagine what you would say and do coming at this experience from each of these two completely different perspectives. Our challenge as parents is to develop our awareness so that we can create a pause in moments like these. The pause gives us the opportunity to make a choice. But here is the key point: It is not just about choosing what to "do" in this situation; it is about first choosing how you are going to "see" this situation—and who you are going to "be" in this situation. Your actions will naturally flow out of your state of mind.

Consider this scenario…You have created an invitation for your son's high school graduation party using a software program you found online. After the design is complete, you print the invitation for one final proofread. As you are reviewing it, you notice that the date of the party is wrong. So you grab an eraser, erase the incorrect date and write in the correct date. Feeling a sense of relief that the project is done you reprint the final version of the invitation. Lo and behold, the version you just printed still has the incorrect date on it. Perplexed, you grab the eraser and repeat the process. After three attempts, you throw up your hands in frustration and give up

Obviously, the only way to correct the printout is to correct it at the source. You must update the date in the source document on your computer.

Now let's extend this analogy to your life.

Let's say you have a goal of improving your health through eating better and exercising. You lay out a plan for the week that includes healthy meals and getting up one hour earlier than normal so you can work out at your local gym. When your alarm goes off one hour earlier on Monday morning, however, you hit the snooze button and say to yourself that you will start tomorrow. Also, since you are not starting the new workout routine until tomorrow there is no need to follow the healthy menu until tomorrow as well.

Does this sound familiar?

Consider this perspective: Your actions are a printout of your thoughts and mindset. They are a reflection of what is going on inside of you. Consequently, your attempts to change your results by focusing on changing your actions are like erasing and correcting the date on the printed invitation. While you may be able to change your actions for a day, a week, or even a month, eventually your actions will revert back to reflect their source: your mindset.

So, if you want more than temporary improvement, start with the source code. Start with your mindset and perspective. Focus your attention on what is going on inside of you.

Identify the thoughts that don't support your ideal life. As you become more aware of your limiting thoughts and beliefs, you will be in a position to make a choice.

Back to Bri and her "horrible" teacher. From a love-based mindset, I found myself focused on two opportunities for growth. First, there was an opportunity to encourage Brianne to be compassionate. We (my wife and I) introduced the possibility of this teacher going through a difficult time in their personal life. We emphasized the point that people are fundamentally good and want to feel a sense of purpose with their work. If this teacher was mean or seemed uninspired, then the loving response would involve a compassionate act of kindness. It could be as simple as a nice smile and saying good morning as she walked into class.

Next, we pointed out that this wouldn't be the last time she was faced with an obstacle between her and one of her goals. One of her most valuable skills would be the ability to come up with a plan to overcome the inevitable obstacles she would face the rest of high school or in college. Then we shifted into coaching mode and asked some open-ended questions:

- Where else could you get help with the class?
- What would happen if you went and talked to the teacher?
- What about starting a study group with some other kids in the class?

Within 15 minutes, she seemed in a much better place. Interestingly, she didn't lay out a specific plan with us, but I could tell she had a pretty good idea of what she was going to do.

After this initial conversion we didn't hear much more about this particular "horrible" teacher. We checked in a couple of times, but she said it was going great so we didn't dig any deeper. Bri did somehow survive this class, but more importantly she moved a few more steps along her internal journey of personal growth.

Insight #3—Outside influences: The big secret

You may be saying to yourself, "Yeah, I can see the value of choosing the love-based approach of empowerment. And I can see how through practice I could develop my ability to intentionally choose empowerment even when my buttons are getting pushed. But the problem is that my teenager is being bombarded with 'bad' advice and influence. There are their friends, social media, the videos they watch, the music they listen to. I am just one voice. How am I supposed to overcome all of these other messages?"

There is a simple answer to this question. You can definitely overcome all of these outside influences because you are the mother or the father of your teenager. And as the parent, you are the most influential relationship they will ever have. There is a story from the book *Staying Connected to Your Teenager* by Michael Riera, PhD, that illustrates this point.

The story is about a common theme Riera experienced at workshops he would lead for teenagers. These workshops were designed to help the teenage participants with communication skills and self-image. One of the exercises involved having the teens develop a list of commitments. The task was to create a list of the actions or goals that were most important to them right now. After the lists were completed, Riera would have the participants share their top three commitments with the rest of the group.

Over the many years that Riera led these workshops, he noticed a pattern when it came time to share their top three commitments. The first few brave souls would talk about going to college, doing some community service, or getting more involved with their church. But eventually one of the teenagers would say that their top commitment was to be kinder to their parents. The interesting dynamic was that after the first time this was mentioned, the majority of the teens that followed included being nicer to their parents on their list of top three commitments. Riera went on to describe how the teenagers acknowledged that their parents loved them and then they would list all of the ways parents supported them. Helping with homework. Driving them to band practice. Paying the equipment fee for the football team. But for some reason they, the teenagers, were (to use their words) "jerks" to their parents.

At the end of this section, Riera shares what happened with one particular student named Ronnie. After Ronnie declared his commitment to be nice to his parents, he said this:

"But the crazy thing is that even though I want to go home and treat them better, I know that I won't. I'm not sure why, I just know that not much will change. Hey, I'm just being honest. So, my commitment is that by the time I graduate, I'll let them know how much I appreciate and love them, even if I have to write it on a card."

Riera closes out this section by making this important statement:

"No matter what else you take from this book, please take away this last point:

You and your opinions matter deeply to your teenagers. During adolescence, they probably will never tell you this directly, but it's still true."

Maybe the best way to understand this is to reflect on your own relationship with your parents. How was your relationship with your parents during your teen years? If you were to have been given the time to reflect like the teens from these workshops —to stop and consider what was most important—where would you have ranked your relationship with your parents? Not the quality of the relationship, but the importance or impact of the relationship?

Whether you realize it or not, you are the most influential person in your teenager's life.

You may be thinking, "How could a teenager who claims to hate their parents really want to heal the relationship?" Well, could it be that the intensity is because their relationship with their parents is so important? Could it be that they are overwhelmed with fear and just don't know what to do?

You may be wondering how the sweet child you have been living with for the first twelve years of their life could become so difficult. Could it be that they are starting to see themselves as independent or separate from their parents and this is a scary place to be?

You may be thinking that you just need to wait until they grow out of this. Consider this, though: If your teenager's relationship with their mom and dad is broken, could this have an impact on their relationships with friends, teachers, and coaches? By building connection with your teenager, you are giving them the skills to deepen the connection in all of their other relationships as well.

You may be wondering how teachers and other adults seem to have a completely different view of your teenager. They tell you how respectful and helpful they are. Could it be that when your teenager is out in the world, they work hard at controlling their actions, and when they get home—in a safe space—they are able to let their guard down and allow all of the negative energy to come flowing out? They expect you, their parents, to accept them as they are. They expect you to be the one person who loves them unconditionally and will never give up on them.

Let me ask you a couple of questions:

Can you see that your teenager is longing to deepen their relationship with you? Can you see how exercising your power to choose—and always responding with love and acting with the intention to empower—could be the greatest gift you could ever give your child?

Part 3: Transformation—Skills and Strategies

To transform your relationship with your teenager, we are going to focus on three fundamental processes.

- Shifting your mindset—choosing love over fear in the moment
- Building connection with your teenager
- Empowering your teenager to be their absolute best

While these three processes are interconnected and many times will seemingly be happening simultaneously, there is an order to them.

Think of it this way:

Before you can empower your teenager to be their absolute best you have to develop a strong connection with them.

But before you can build a strong connection, you have to be grounded in love-based principles, values, and beliefs.

Consequently, the foundation for building connection with your teenager and empowering them to be their absolute best is built on your ability to intentionally choose and stay grounded in a love-based mindset.

Of course, there is a big difference between knowing about a love-based mindset, building connection, and being a source of empowerment and actually putting these ideas into practice. Reading the following sections will help to provide insights, ideas, and inspiration, but there is no substitute for real-life experience. I am inviting you to be okay with feeling uncomfortable and awkward. Commit to staying the course and you will have those *aha* moments. Moments when you really get the power of love in a way that you never knew was possible.

This is the difference between knowledge and wisdom—the space where miracles happen.

Section 1: Shifting Your Mindset to Choosing Love Over Fear

Over the next several pages we are going to explore the process of shifting your mindset to choose love over fear. This is the foundation—a prerequisite—for transforming your relationship with your teenager from one of control to one of empowerment.

Note: If you commit to doing the work necessary to become more self-aware and intentional about choosing your mindset, the processes of building connection and empowering your teenager will naturally follow. For some, this process can be difficult, but keep in mind that those of you who are the most stuck—and the most skeptical— are the ones poised for the biggest breakthroughs. Also, keep in mind that the fact that you are undertaking this effort shows you are exactly where you are supposed to be along your journey of personal and parenting growth.

Let's start off by taking a high-level look at how we typically engage with events in our lives:

Step one: The stimulus. Something happens.
Step two: You interpret this circumstance based on your past.
Step three: You experience emotions surrounding the circumstance.

Step four: You respond.

Here is a simple example of how this looks in your everyday life:

Step one: (stimulus) Your teenager forgets to set their alarm so they wake up late and miss the bus.
Step two: (interpretation) You immediately think that they are irresponsible and being inconsiderate because now you are going to have to take them to school, which will make you late to work.
Step three: (emotional experience) You feel a strong sense of frustration and anger.
Step four: (response) The natural response that flows from your anger and frustration is yelling at your teenager combined with looks of disappointment.

Our focus is going to be steps two and three. How you interpret or perceive any stimulus and the related emotional experience. If you are struggling with your teenager, I can guarantee you that your interpretations are rooted in a fear-based mindset. For many of you, responding from a fear-based mindset has become a habit. It is automatic.

Here is an alternative process for you to work toward:

Step one: The stimulus. Something happens.
Step two: You interpret this circumstance based on your past.
Step three: You have an emotional experience surrounding the circumstance.
New Step: You create a pause.
New Step: Through self-awareness you evaluate your emotional experience as either fear based or love based.
New Step: You state your intention based on your mindset.

New Step: You reinterpret the circumstance based on your stated intention.
New Step: You have a transformed emotional experience.
Step four: You respond.

You may have seen this process represented like this:

Stimulus  Response

Change or transformation happens when you create a pause.

Stimulus  Pause  Response

During this pause, you have the opportunity to introduce self-awareness, intention, and choice.

Let's take a look at some strategies and techniques for these new steps, breaking them into two distinct phases: the *reflection phase* and the *action phase*.

In the *reflection phase*, I am going to ask you to take some time to reflect and develop goals for yourself and your family. I am going to challenge you to articulate your vision for your family. We are going to explore new habits and strategies for being intentional. To use a sports analogy, this is kind of like designing a game plan, practicing the plays, and developing the physical skills and strength needed to play the game.

The *action phase* involves the development of strategies for making adjustments in the heat of the moment. I am going to teach you how to create a pause when life is putting the squeeze on you and show you how to use this pause as an opportunity to shift your perspective and uncover new courses of action. To continue the sports analogy, this is kind of like making halftime adjustments.

Reflection phase:

For this phase, we are going to focus on the following areas:

- Mastering the topic
- Vision for family
- Triggers—Used for good.
- Transitions—Setting your intention
- Daily and weekly self-assessment

Mastering the topic:

In order to clarify the distinction between being grounded in love and grounded in fear, we will start with identifying the principles, values, and beliefs that reside at the core of each perspective.

Here are the core beliefs that make up a *loving* perspective:

- Love heals: Forgiveness, gratitude, and compassion are the foundation for healing.
- Law of attraction: What you focus your attention on grows.
- Life is abundant.
- Purpose: All people have a contribution to make and the ability to make a difference.
- All actions are either an expression of love or a call for love: Love is always the answer.

- We are empowered to choose our perspective: A change in perspective can change everything.
- Truth is important: Integrity is the path to peace.
- We are one body: True connection can only happen in the present moment.
- Life is a journey: Value or a greater purpose can be found in all circumstances.
- People are fundamentally good: We must work to bring this out in ourselves and others.

Alternatively, here are the core beliefs that make up a *fearful* perspective:

- We are all alone and separate.
- I am a victim of my circumstances.
- I am not worthy of the love of others.
- I have to protect myself from others and hide my flaws and faults.
- Bad things happen for no apparent reason.
- The sources of happiness are outside of my control.
- Life is a zero-sum game. For every winner there is a loser.
- People (myself, my teenager) are fundamentally bad or flawed.

Which of these two lists do you relate to more?

Please note that it is perfectly normal for both of these belief systems to reside inside of you. Through our upbringing and the influence of our culture, we are taught both sets of principles, values, and beliefs. Unfortunately, for many, the fearful perspective starts to take over and in some cases completely overshadows the love-based beliefs that allow us to make an intentional choice. So, the first step is to reestablish an awareness of the core principles, values, and beliefs that make up a loving perspective. The goal is to bring these beliefs forward in your mind, increasing your awareness of the choice you have between a love-based thought system and a fear-based thought system.

Next, set aside 15 minutes in a quiet place for reflection.

Step one: Identify a difficult situation or exchange between you and your teenager that happened within the last few days.

Step two: Close your eyes and take yourself back to what transpired, but this time as an observer, not a participant.

Step three: Ask yourself the following questions:

- What emotions are you experiencing?
- Are you engaging from a fear-based mindset or a love-based mindset?
- How can you tell the difference?
- What core belief or beliefs from the list above is driving the emotions you are experiencing and your actions?

Now, repeat this exercise with a different circumstance. This time choose a pleasant or "good" exchange between you and your teenager, and ask yourself the same series of questions. It is likely that you have some different answers this time.

Here is a stretch project. In your journal or on a piece of paper, start your own list of fear-based and love-based principles, values, and beliefs. Use the list I provided above as a starting point. Feel free to rephrase the ones that don't speak directly to you. Add new ones that come to mind as you do the reflection exercise.

Again, this is all about self-awareness.

Vision for family:

Do you have a vision statement for your family? What is your ultimate goal?

As I stated earlier, my definition of a *successful family* encapsulates my vision statement for our family:

A *successful family* is one whose members speak with respect, honor difference, provide a nurturing environment, empower each other, and truly enjoy being together.

This family has a knack for really enjoying and appreciating the good times, while at the same time, they can effectively deal with any difficult issues that come their way. There is a sense of peace, joy, warmth, and love within their home.

If you don't have a vision statement for your family, I highly recommend taking some time to reflect on how you would define "success." Include the whole family in this process. Ask these questions:

- How should we treat each other?
- What would you like to feel when you are at home or around the rest of the family?
- What should our family stand for?
- How would you like to be able to describe our family?

You may be surprised by how thoughtful your teenager can be.

As a family, write out a vision statement that captures these ideals. Print it out. Frame it and hang it in your home. This statement should become your family's north star. Set the example by acknowledging that there is a gap between where you are in your personal development and where you need to be in order to achieve this vision. State your commitment to ongoing growth.

Note: A growth mindset can be very powerful. It establishes the reality that change for the better is possible. A commitment to ongoing personal growth is the cornerstone for HOPE.

Triggers—Used for good

For many people, the word "trigger" has a negative connotation, bringing to mind certain people who know how to push your buttons, pet peeves, or even traumatic events from your past.

For our purposes, I am going to recommend that you establish some love-based triggers in your life. Here are some examples:

- Set up alarms on your phone or computer with love-based quotes or phrases. How about an alarm that goes off at 10:00 a.m. and 3:00 p.m. with the phrase, "Love is always the answer"?
- Every time you walk into a building, say, "I will be a source of joy."
- Whenever someone provides an act of service for you, look them in the eye and thank them.
- When you see a group of teenagers, in your mind send some love and positive energy their way. Say to yourself: *You are loved and you make a difference.*

You get the idea. Take 15 minutes to reflect and come up with a few love-based triggers that you can incorporate into your daily life. The goal is to continue to bring your love-based thought system into your awareness and develop the habit of engaging with the world from a loving perspective.

Transitions—Setting your intention

When you step back and look at your day, you will notice that it was full of transitions. These are the times when you are moving from one activity or environment to another. For example: When you move from your daily routine for getting ready in the morning to the process of getting everyone out the door on time; when you move from your car after your commute into your office; when you walk back into the house after a work day ;or when you pick your teenager up after practice and they get in the car.

I am going to recommend that you take some time to reflect on how you can be more intentional about the opportunity these transitions present. Here is what I mean. Take the time to plan out and state your intention in preparation for a typical transition that happens every day. Let's say your teenager gets home every day at 4:15. Reflect on how you want their first 15 minutes at home to go and develop an intention statement you can say to yourself at 4:10. How about:

When Rachel walks in the door, I am going to greet her with love. If she wants to talk, I am going to be present and just listen with compassion. If she doesn't want to talk, I will not take it personally. I will just be present and available to her.

What you are doing is establishing your mindset. If it has been a particularly difficult day for you, close your eyes, take a few deep breaths, and feel the release of any negative energy. As the negativity dissipates, move to your intention statement and feel yourself being filled with loving energy. Now you are ready for the transition.

Can you see how these regular transitions could become a planned "trigger"?

Here is your challenge. Take 15 minutes to consider one or two regular daily transitions. Pick the one that seems to be the most difficult for you and your teenager. Write out an intention statement. For the next week, be very intentional about setting your mindset as the transition approaches.

If you forget or miss a day, consider it part of your practice. Part of your journey. The goal is to make being intentional a habit. Make it a part of who you are as a person. This can only happen if you give yourself grace and stay the course.

Daily and weekly self-assessment

The final practice for this phase involves regular self-assessment accomplished through journaling.

Daily assessment:

Take a few minutes at the end of your day to review your progress. Here are a few prompts to get the process started.

Did I experience fear-based emotions today?

- What were they?
- How did I feel physically?

- What action did I take?
- What was the underlying principle, value, or belief?

Did I experience any love-based emotions today?

- What were they?
- How did I feel physically?
- What action did I take?
- What was the underlying principle, value or belief?

How did my transitions go today?

- Did I state my intention?
- If yes, did I notice any shift in my ability to connect or empower my teenager?
- What happened after I made the transition?

Did I encounter any of my love-based triggers today?

What are three things that happened today I am grateful for?

I highly recommend getting a journal or writing out your thoughts in a word-processing program or a notes app on your phone. There is something about the process of writing out your thoughts that helps you crystalize them. This also creates a record of your progress over time, giving a before and after picture.

End the assessment process each day by reviewing your vision for your family.

<u>Weekly assessment:</u>

Each week, go back and review the prior week's entries. Look for any patterns, such as certain times of the day that are a struggle or times that always seem to go well, negative triggers that keep popping up, or certain days of the week that are always better or worse than others. Then look ahead to the next week. Identify any potential issues and set some goals for the week.

- What would I like to focus on this week?
- Do we have anything going on this week that I need to be mindful of?
- What would be a win for this week?
- If you identify a negative pattern, ask: How else could I look at this? Or what would work better here?

Self-assessment is a critical part of personal development and family enrichment. Many of your greatest insights will come during these times of quiet reflection.

Action phase:

Now we are going to explore a process for changing your perspective in the heat of the moment, resulting in more positive and intentional actions.

Step one involves developing your awareness so you get better at recognizing when you are seeing the world from a loving perspective versus when you are not. I have found that the easiest way to recognize your mindset is to pay attention to your emotional experience. For example, if you are experiencing any of these emotions, you are NOT seeing the world from a loving perspective:

- Anger
- Frustration
- Disappointment
- Apathy
- Fear
- Overwhelm

The goal here is to catch ourselves in the moment so that we can create a pause. It is this pause that will give us the opportunity to make an intentional choice to see the circumstance from a different perspective.

If you are struggling with your self-awareness, start by observing other people. See if you can catch someone being pulled into a state of frustration or anger by a particular circumstance. For example: On a particularly busy day at my favorite bagel restaurant, I witnessed an onslaught of frustration and anger. At this restaurant, you order at the counter and then wait for your name to be called. As I was enjoying my bagel at my table, I noticed that one man had been waiting for a while. The person behind the counter called another name that was not his. As this other person walked up to pick up their order, I could see this man's disposition change. You could see it in his face and in his body language. He was beset with frustration. On this day, he became overwhelmed with these unloving emotions and responded by yelling at the employee who was working the cash register.

As you watch events like this unfold, you will be developing your ability to recognize when you are the one being pulled into the darkness of an unloving perspective.

So step one is to catch yourself in the middle of a state of frustration, disappointment, or any of these emotions that indicate you are seeing the world from an unloving perspective, and then create a pause and explore this idea:

- I have a choice.: I can continue to view this circumstance from an unloving perspective or I can follow the steps to shift to a loving perspective. What do I want to do right now?

The answer to this question becomes your stated intention.

You may want to write this question down and carry it with you so you can pull it out when you catch yourself in one of these moments. I recommend reading it aloud. There is something effective about actually hearing yourself say these words. If you choose to make the shift to a loving perspective, here is a process that will guide you through the transition.

I am going to use the bagel restaurant circumstance from before to illustrate how this process works. This process is centered around three questions.

Change your life with three simple questions:

Although I am going to continue to use the bagel incident to illustrate, I have found that participants get more value when they also follow along with an example from their own life.

Start by taking a moment to identify a circumstance that happened to you in the last few days where you experienced one of the emotions that signal an unloving perspective. For the purpose of this exercise, I recommend that you choose a situation that bothered you but wasn't too overwhelming or emotional.

Okay, take a few minutes and write down what happened, how you felt, and what you did. Come back when you are done.

GO!

Before we move on, I have a question: As you sat there reflecting, were you experiencing any of the same emotions you did when this particular circumstance was playing out? Did this exercise of writing down what happened stir up the emotions again?

When I do this exercise with participants in my live workshops, most everyone experiences a return of the original emotions. Interestingly, these events are hours or even days removed and yet our thoughts, interpretations, and perceptions can bring back an emotional response. So, consider whether it was the events that made you feel that way or your perception of the event.

Now that you have your circumstance in mind, write down the answers to these questions:

Question 1: What was wrong?

In the incident at the bagel shop, the man would say that it was not right or fair that other people were receiving their food before him, as he was there first and ordered first.

Question 2: Who/what was to blame?

There was a lot of blame to go around in the bagel shop that morning. The poor management of the restaurant, the incompetent employee at the cash register, the profit-focused company that refused to hire enough people to handle the morning rush, etc.

Question 3: How did or how could you protect your own interests?

Our hungry restaurant patron chose to protect himself by yelling at the employees behind the counter, demanding his money back, and swearing that he would never come back.

Take a few minutes and answer each of these questions for the circumstance you describe.

GO!

These three questions reflect the way we typically respond to the difficult issues or circumstances that we encounter in life. These questions represent *a fear-based mindset.*

Now here are the three questions that will create the shift to *a love-based mindset*:

Question 1: Who/what did I need to forgive?

In the case of the bagel incident, the customer could let go of his frustration and forgive the employees.

Question 2: What could I be grateful for?

Again, the man at the bagel shop that morning could have focused on the fact that someone had gotten up at 3:00 a.m. to come in and bake the bagel that he was about to eat. This person got out of a warm bed in order to be of service to him and many others on this day.

Question 3: How could I have made a difference?

Finally, there was an opportunity to support the struggling staff that morning. Instead of standing there being frustrated, he could have used the time to clean up the coffee station as an act of charity. Or he could have offered some compassionate words to another waiting customer.

Take a few minutes to reflect on your circumstance and answer these three questions.

If you are up to it, I would challenge you to answer question 3, but this time in the present tense. Not what could you have done, but what can you still do? Then follow through and execute the action. I would like to introduce the idea of charity here. The answer to the question "How can I make a difference?" is an act of charity. It is a gift to be given freely.

When you do this, don't be surprised by the sense of purpose, the joy, or the boost of energy you experience. Remember: To give is to receive.

See if this speaks to you. The shift from a fear-based mindset to a love-based mindset is accomplished by shifting from a "me" focus to an "other" focus. Instead of focusing on your unfulfilled needs, shift to how you can serve others, focusing on compassion, forgiveness, gratitude, and charity.

Section 2: Nine Ways to Build Connection

As we begin to closely consider how to build connections with those we love, especially our teenagers, it seems appropriate to share a few thoughts on the nature of love itself. First of all, the word love has a few different meanings or uses. One of the most common is love as an emotion. Like feeling sad or feeling happy, we can feel love. I like to think of this as the physical experience of love. It feels a certain way to us...it feels good. Next, love is often used as a verb. It is something that you do. "I love you" implies some action. You might say that someone is a loving person. Again this implies some kind of action on their part. At the same time, I have heard people refer to love as a possession. They will say, "She has a lot of love in her heart" or " I only have some much love to give." It is not that one of these meanings is right and the others are wrong, it is just the use of one word to represent different, but certainly related, ideas.

For our purposes, I see love as a noun. It is a thing,—more precisely, an energy. It is kind of like a radio transmission. Love is a signal that we can tune into. When we do, we see the world differently. We feel different; we act differently. To continue this analogy, I would assert that the love "signal" is always there—it is just that we are often tuned to a different station. So this brings us back to my earlier assertion: We have the ability to choose our perspective, or you could say that we have the ability to choose which signal we tune into.

Imagine that it is a lazy Saturday morning and as a treat you decide to go to the local coffee shop and splurge on a $5 cup of coffee. As you are walking out, you hear the cry of a small child. It is a little girl who appears to be five or six years old. She is sitting on the ground crying. She is by herself and looks scared. What is your instinctive response?

She is lost...she is afraid...she is alone....she is disconnected from her mom and dad. Wouldn't you agree that this situation calls for a loving response? Does it make sense to get mad at her for being lost? Should we be disappointed in her for being afraid?

Now, let's fast forward 10 years. Now she is 15 or 16. Could she ever feel lost? Could she ever feel alone and afraid? Could she ever feel disconnected from her mom and dad?

Could it be that all of your teenager's "bad" behavior—the stuff that doesn't line up with our definition of a *successful person*—is just an attempt to deal with the fear of being disconnected, left out, or isolated?

Could it be that your teenager senses that something is not right but is not sure why and doesn't know how to communicate what is going on?

Could it be that they are calling out for your love in the only way they can right at this moment?

Think of it this way: Love heals separation and creates connection.

Here are a couple of examples of the kinds of circumstances that your teenager is confronted with

Back when my oldest daughter was a sophomore in high school, my wife and I volunteered to help at the homecoming dance. I was given the job of door man at one of the two doors the kids would be entering the dance through. After the initial rush of people coming in, the second part of my job was to make sure no one was going out and then coming back into the dance. At this particular entrance, there was a set of outside doors, a large vestibule, and then another set of doors that led into the school. During the initial rush, I noticed a young man who made his way into the vestibule but was waiting by the outside door. He had the look of a freshman. (If you go to any high school you will notice that most of the time it is pretty easy to distinguish between the freshmen and seniors.) He had on a jacket and tie and was holding a box from a local flower shop. Forty-five minutes later, the rush of kids entering the dance had passed and he and I were the only two people left standing in the vestibule. At this point, I could tell he was getting a little uneasy about his predicament. Keep in mind that this was at a time where not every teenager had a cell phone. Another hour passed and still no date arrived. By this time, it was apparent that the young woman who said she would meet him at the dance was not going to show up. I couldn't help but wonder if he was going to tell his parents what happened and if he did, how they would respond. And how was this going to play out on Monday when he walked back into the school? Then another thought hit me: How would I respond if I was the parent of the young woman who said yes but then stood up the young man? This is an example of the kinds of circumstances all teenagers are facing every day. Here are a few more:

- Walking into the lunch room and not seeing any of their friends
- Getting a bad grade on a test
- Not getting the part they wanted in the school play
- Getting the part they wanted in the school play and then worrying about what everyone is going to say about their performance
- Getting a good enough grade in a class but deep down knowing they could have done better
- Not making the baseball team
- Getting into an accident two weeks after getting their driver's license.

The list could go on and on. My point is that this is a time in your teen's life where there is a lot going on. They are excited about the idea of independence while at the same time afraid that they won't have what it takes to be successful, make friends, and be accepted. This uncertainty creates a lot of emotions and negative energy for them to process. Now here is a very important point: Unlike a 5- or 6-year-old, most of the time your 15-year-old won't sit on the sidewalk and cry. So what do they do instead when they are feeling overwhelmed with the fear of not belonging or being isolated?

- Overreact to a minor inconvenience
- Pick a fight with a sibling
- Become apathetic toward school
- Experiment with drugs or alcohol
- Lose their appetite because they are nervous about a test in school
- Withdraw into their phone

Again, the list could go on and on. But when you look from a loving perspective, you will recognize that at the core all of this "bad" behavior is a call to connect. A call for love.

Here is another point to consider. Let's go back to the little girl who is lost and afraid. While she is overwhelmed with the emotions of being lost and alone, she is not in a position to effectively take in or receive any advice or coaching on how to handle the situation next time. The first priority is to help her feel safe so that the negative emotional energy dissipates.

This same observation is true for our teenagers—actually, it is true for all of us. If your teenager is experiencing fear or negative emotional energy, they are not in the position to readily receive any of your advice, coaching, or wisdom.

In light of this, building a loving connection is the first priority. In fact, many families have reported that as they work to improve the connection with their teenager, the "bad" behaviors start going away.

Much like the overall goal of building a *successful family*, your connection with your teenager will be ever evolving. There will be good days and bad days. I invite you to think of any "bad" behavior as a gift. It is a signal that your connection has been damaged by something. You may not know what caused the damage, but you can be confident that damage has been done.

Choosing a loving perspective changes everything.

This call for love could also be expressed as a call to connect. All of us want to feel connected or to have a circle of people where we feel accepted and safe. Our family and our home offer the ideal environment for building connections. The challenge with teenagers, though, is that they have a desire to see themselves as separate while at the same time long to be connected. Our goal has always been to create a loving environment at home. A place where our children would feel safe and loved. The connection to us as their parents serves two roles. First, it provides a safe place for our teenagers to regroup and recharge as they navigate the challenges they face every day. Second, a loving connection with their family and a strong sense of home provides a reference point for them to compare new relationships and new environments.

Here is an example:

One aspect of parenting teenagers is the inevitable arrival of boyfriends and girlfriends. This first relationship is like a right of passage. As parents these relationships can present a whole host of challenges, especially if we don't approve of this new person who our teenager is spending all of their time with. If we have established a strong connection and a loving environment at home, however, our teenager will have a point of reference. Our loving relationship becomes the standard they will use to compare this new romantic relationship. They will be able to easily recognize unloving actions or words. While they may not be able to put into words what they are experiencing, they will feel uncomfortable in an unloving environment and will make a decision to return home.

With all of this in mind, I've developed a list of nine effective ways to build connection with your teenager:

1. Being playful
2. Being compassionate
3. Being present

4. Being vulnerable
5. Being a source of hope
6. Being forgiving
7. Being curious
8. Being grateful
9. Being kind

Let's take a look at them one by one.

Being playful:

Being playful seems to come easily when our children are young. Playing hide-and-seek with a three-year-old seems natural. But as our children get older, the playfulness can be lost. Let's take a look at some ways to be playful with your teenager.

My wife and youngest daughter are playful with music. In particular, they love show tunes. During my daughter's high school years, I would walk into the kitchen to find my daughter doing homework at the kitchen table and my wife rearranging the food in the pantry. The food didn't really need to be rearranged, but this was a way to stay in the kitchen. The soundtrack from *Hamilton* or *Les Misérables* would be playing and they would be singing. During the dramatic parts, they would pause what they were doing and the intensity of the singing would grow to the point where I could hear them out in the backyard. Sometimes they would even dance or act out the scene as in the show. When a song would end, no words needed to be said; they would just look at each other and smile.

For me, most of the time I found that a ball was the focus of my playful time. For example: My oldest son played baseball in middle school and through high school. We spent countless hours in the backyard playing catch. Also, with six children, it was not uncommon for a game of two-on-two basketball to break out on the driveway. Physical play also provides a great way for parents and kids to engage in physical touch without it feeling weird. It can be a high-five, a fist bump, or some roughhousing during friendly competition.

Here are some other ideas for being playful with your teenager:

- Video games
- Cards or board games
- Dancing
- Playing music together
- Telling jokes
- Just acting goofy or silly

You get the idea. Play is a great way to engage with your teenager because the only objective is to have fun. It brings back the feeling of when your teen was a child. Another benefit of being playful is that you will feel better. You will feel connected. You might even feel a little younger.

You don't stop playing because you grow old…you grow old because you stop playing.

Being compassionate:

Being compassionate with your teenager is very similar to two of the coaching skills we will explore later: acknowledging and validating. The premise is to relate to your teenager from their perspective. To see the world and their struggles through their eyes. The challenge for us as parents is to resist the urge to pass judgment on whatever is going on for our teen. For example:

Your 15-year-old daughter arrives home from her second day of school freshman year with a sad look on her face. When you ask if everything is okay, she bursts into tears. After a few minutes of consoling she regains her composure enough to tell you what happened at school. As she was walking through the halls between classes, she saw two other girls wearing the same top that she was wearing. This is the moment where we have to be careful to listen without passing judgment. Remember that the goal is to build your connection with her. If you launch into a lecture about how she needs to be more confident in herself or, worse, if you smile and say, "Well, that is ridiculous," she will stomp out of the room screaming, "No one in this house understands how hard it is to be in high school!" Again, being compassionate is about seeing this circumstance from her perspective. Her upset is real for her. The opportunity to empower her and move her along her journey of personal growth into a *successful person* will come later. For now, it is about communicating that she is safe and she is loved. A compassionate response can go a long way in a situation like this. Offer to brush her hair until she feels better. Say something along the lines of, "That sounds like it was awful for you," or "I can tell this is really upsetting," Notice that while these responses are comforting, you are not approving or disapproving of her reaction. You are just being with her in the moment without judgment.

We all want to be heard. We all want to be accepted for who we are. Healing and growth can't happen until we are in the presence of unconditional love. This is true for us. This is especially true for your children.

"We can't heal the world today, but we can begin with a voice of compassion, a heart of love, and an act of kindness."

—Mary Davis

Being present:

In today's world, being present has become a lost art. There are so many distractions and ways for our attention to be drawn away from the people sitting right in front of us. In fact, this is one of the most common issues parents have with their teenagers. Today's teens seem to always have their earbuds in, their computer on, or their attention on their phone. If we are honest with ourselves, we see that we are just as guilty as our teens. We are distracted by work, social media, short news cycles, and easy access to all kinds of entertainment. In today's world, in order to get some quality time with a teenager, parents have to be creative as well as aware of the opportunities to "be with" your teens when they present themselves.

Here is a creative approach I heard from one mom. She had read that teens were more likely to open up and talk late at night. Every once in a while, she would say good night to her teenage son and head up to bed. She would set her alarm to wake up at 1:00 a.m. Then she would wander downstairs. Once she was downstairs she would tell her son she was having trouble falling asleep and would start making herself a snack. Naturally she would offer to make her son something as well. If he was playing a video game, she would sit down next to him with her snack and say something like, "Who is winning?" Then just wait. The goal here is to stay present with no agenda. She reported that not always but more often than not, he would share a story about one of his classes or something that happened at school. After a little while, she would say, "I need to try to get some sleep. Good night, son." These late night talks were a great way to hear about what was going on in her son's life.

Every once in a while your teen will initiate the conversation. Now, don't expect them to walk up and say, "Hey Mom, can we talk?" It will be much more subtle, and most of the time it will be at the most inopportune moment. It is up to us to pick up on their interest in talking, drop what we are doing, and just be present and listen. Here is an example: My youngest daughter, Isabella, worked as a waitress during high school. One night in the summer after her senior year in high school she strolled in after a dinner shift at around 11:00 with a bag of food. I happened to be in the kitchen, which was unusual, because I am more of a morning person and usually in bed by 10:00. As she plopped down and started to eat she said, "What are you doing up?" I responded, "Mom and I started a movie around 9:00 and it just finished." Then I asked how her night was. Normally, her response to this question was to say "fine" and then pull out her phone, but on this night she said, "It was okay, I guess. Some people can be so difficult." At this point I could have said, "Yeah, I know… Well, goodnight" and gone up to bed. I was tired and it was past my bedtime. Fortunately, I recognized this as an invitation to talk, so instead I said, "What do you mean when you say people can be so difficult?" (a clarifying question) At this point she launched into the details of her night, so I sat down at the table with her and just listened. Twenty minutes later she had finished the food she brought home and said she was going to go to bed. The hardest part for me was to resist the urge to offer advice or fix what I saw as problems. At this moment the goal was to just be present and let her know that she was being heard.

Interestingly, as you develop your ability to be present and experience a few quality moments with your teen, they will start naturally becoming more available to you. It feels good to connect with someone who loves you unconditionally, and I would assert that no matter how mean, aloof, or disapproving your teen appears to be, they long to be connected with you.

Being vulnerable:

Many parents underestimate the benefits of being vulnerable with their teenagers. During their teenage years, your child is faced with new challenges every day and while they may try to act like they have it all together, underneath there is uncertainty and fear about their abilities. There is the constant questioning and wondering if they have what it takes. This is where your vulnerability comes into play. When you share your fears and concerns, your teenager will realize that they are not alone and that it is natural to feel some doubt when they are faced with new or difficult challenges. Vulnerability is one of the best ways to affirm that personal growth is good, that growth can be scary, and that growth is a lifelong process that should be embraced.

Here is an example of being vulnerable:

As your 12-year-old son or daughter moves into their teenage years, they will seemingly transform into a different person. They will start expressing their individuality and independence, coming home with their hair dyed green and challenging you regarding your principles, values, and beliefs. During this time, your role as the parent will transition into unfamiliar territory. This transition is an opportunity to be vulnerable while demonstrating to your teen the importance of personal growth.

During a moment when you sense a strong connection to your teen, say something like this:

"I have been meaning to mention something to you, and this seems like a good time. Being a teenager is new territory for you. While it is exciting to experience newfound independence, it can also be a little overwhelming. I just want you to know that this is new territory for me as well. Being the parent of a teenager. While I am excited to see you grow into a young adult, I know there are going to be times when I will not be sure what to do. To be honest, this is a little scary for me. It is scary because the stakes are higher now. I mean, when you were five, not only did I know all of your friends, I knew your friends' parents. If one of them was being mean or doing something that might hurt you, it was easy for me to jump in and help. During high school, you are going to meet a lot of new people who I will not know. While this is exciting, for me it is a big change. I already can tell that it is going to be hard for me to know when I should step in and help and when I should give you a little space. I just want you to know that I love you no matter what and I am committed to learning and growing to be the best parent I can for you."

What do you think? How do you think your teen would respond if you had this conversation?

I'll tell you, I have been a parent for 35 years now, and I can say with absolute certainty that I don't have it all figured out. Every day, my wife and I are faced with new circumstances that challenge us to grow and develop. The purpose of this book is to share what I have learned and to provide opportunities to gain a deeper understanding of the healing power of love.

Here is an eye-opening story I heard during a personal growth program I attended. The facilitator of the workshop was part of Tony Robbins's team of workshop leaders. Through this connection with Tony Robbins, she had an opportunity to participate in a program with a room full of highly successful people, including Oprah Winfrey. At one point in the program, the workshop leader asked everyone in the room to rank their skill and expertise, related to their profession, on a scale from 1 to 10. The *aha* moment came when Oprah announced that she had given herself a 3. How could Oprah, the most successful women in media, say that her level of expertise in professional media is a 3? Oprah went on to say that she has always felt that there was so much more to be learned professionally, and she attributed a large part of her success to a burning desire to always be learning and growing.

David Willis once said, "Growth is often uncomfortable, messy, and full of feelings you weren't expecting." I would add that it is okay to let your kids in on this secret.

Being a source of hope:

Hope is centered on the belief that tomorrow is somehow going to be better than today. Interestingly, in order to experience a sense of hope, you don't have to know the details of how the circumstances are going to change or the plan of action to get from where you are to where you want to be. Hope springs from the belief in the possibility that it can happen. As the parent of a teenager, we become a source of hope by focusing our attention on your child's strengths, gifts, and potential. Think about how awesome you feel when someone acknowledges your abilities, or even more importantly, when they acknowledge a character trait like kindness or a forgiving heart. When teenagers believe in themselves, it will be easier for them to see past a difficult circumstance. The definition of a *successful person* that I shared earlier speaks directly to this: "A successful person has the ability to effectively deal with any difficult circumstances that come their way."

Here are a couple of examples to consider:

Our daughter Isabella worked as a waitress at a local restaurant all through high school and in the summers during college. This restaurant has been a staple in our community for years, and via a visit from the Food Network show *Man v. Food*, it has become a destination for out-of-town visitors. One day in the summer after her freshman year of college, she came home excited to share a story about a particular customer. A father and his adult son were seated in her section. As she typically did, she asked them if they had ever been to Bub's before. The father said that they had not. He went on to say that they actually lived a couple of hours away and they had heard that this was a place they should check out. Isabella said they asked a few questions as the meal progressed and she filled them in on the restaurant's history and a few tidbits on our community. When the meal was done, the father paid with a credit card. Isabella's older sister is in the U.S. Marines, and she noticed the credit card had the Marine emblem on it. When she brought back the check after processing the credit card, she asked if he was a

Marine. She said that they talked for a few minutes and she shared that she had a sister in the Marines as well. When Isabella went back to the table after they had left, she found an awesome surprise. Their total bill was for $60 and they had left her a $100 tip! As you can imagine she was pretty excited. $100 will buy a lot of Starbucks for a college student.

We recognized this as an opportunity to acknowledge some of her strengths. Her mother and I were quick to point out that this didn't happen by accident. She is always very engaging and pleasant with people. Also, we reminded her that she has a great work ethic and we were sure she took great care of them. Then, most importantly, we said that she is really good at connecting with people and making them feel welcome and important. Finally, we told her that no matter what issues or difficult circumstances she faces in her life, this ability to connect combined with her work ethic are going to serve her well.

An additional benefit to pointing out your teen's strengths after a success is that you can reach back to these experiences when your teen is struggling. This is a way to bring hope during a difficult time—when life is putting the squeeze on. For example: If our daughter called home frustrated about the efforts of her assigned partners in a group project for a class, we could easily remind her of ability to engage people and make them feel connected. We could point to the $100 tip story as well as other times when she had success in a similar situation. A great approach is to remind your child of their previous success and the particular strength they possess and then ask an empowerment question, like this:

"You are so good at engaging with others and building relationships. How could that help you and your group work better together?"

When someone believes in themselves and is grounded in love, they will be able to find hope even in the most difficult circumstances.

"Hope is being able to see the light despite all of the darkness."

—Desmond Tutu

Being forgiving:

Forgiveness may be the most powerful way to build connection. Or I should say rebuild connection. Think of it this way. Something happens between two people that damages their relationship. Maybe one of them breaks trust by not doing what they said they would do or by saying something offensive. Forgiveness is always the first step to healing the relationship and rebuilding the connection. This is certainly true with your teen as well. There will be times when you will need to forgive your teen, and there will also be times when you will ask your teen for forgiveness.

Forgiveness can be misunderstood. Many people see forgiveness as a gift that is given to the person who committed the offense. The aggrieved person will delay giving the forgiveness until they feel the other person has made amends for what they have done. They have to apologize and promise to never commit the offensive act again. There are conditions for the forgiveness. With this view of forgiveness, there are also certain actions that are unforgivable.

If this is how you would describe forgiveness, I invite you to consider a different perspective: Forgiveness is a gift to the person who is offering the forgiveness, not the person who committed the offensive act. While withholding our forgiveness until amends are made may feel like we have taken back control or power over the situation, it is in fact the complete opposite. When we treat it this way, our return to joy, regaining our peace of mind, is completely dependent on the actions of the person who committed the offense. We become a victim. What if they never apologize or demonstrate remorse in an acceptable manner? I am sure you know of at least a few examples of family members who haven't spoken with each other for years over some action or words. In these situations, something that happened decades ago can still be causing considerable suffering today. I have heard people say, "I don't know if I can ever forgive them." But there are two issues with the unforgivable. First, if the act is unforgivable, then you will be a victim of the act forever and never be able to fully return to joy, peace of mind, or a sense of purpose. Second, if it is possible to commit an unforgivable act, then in the back of your mind you will believe that it is also possible that someday you yourself could commit such an act, destroying any chance for joy, peace of mind, or sense of purpose.

I realize that this is a weighty conversation to have with teens and adults alike, but I have found over my 40 years as a husband, father, and now grandfather that forgiveness holds the keys to building *successful families*. Here is a distinction for you to consider. Forgiveness is a loving act in response to a call for love. In the same way that teens' bad behavior can be viewed as a call for love, all unloving acts can be viewed as a call for love. Unloving acts are only committed by individuals who are experiencing fear from a sense of being alone, not being accepted, not being good enough, and/or not being important to anyone. Think of forgiveness as clearing your negative judgments about a circumstance—the negative energy—so that you will be in a position to heal the relationship and make a difference. This is a much different view than forgiveness as just the acceptance of an unloving act.

Forgiveness is a topic that could fill a whole book. To close out this brief discussion of forgiveness, I invite you to open up to the possibilities forgiveness brings to your family and your teenager. Model forgiveness for your teenager with all of your relationships. Coach your teen on the power of forgiveness in their relationships within the family as well as with friends.

"We must develop and maintain the capacity to forgive. He who is devoid of the power to forgive is devoid of the power to love."

—Martin Luther King

Being curious:

Learning and discovering new ideas, talents, and concepts is invigorating. Have you ever noticed how curious young children are? They are constantly exploring and trying new things. I would assert that curiosity is a natural part of being a human being. Unfortunately, as adults, we get too busy with the everyday details of living our lives and we push our natural curiosity to the side. I invite you to approach your teenager with genuine curiosity. What is it like to be a teenager today? What are they going through? How do they view the world? The challenge is to resist the urge to immediately judge everything you discover. If you can develop the ability to ask the questions without being confrontational, you will be letting them know that they have been heard and that their experiences, thoughts, and feelings have value.

I know what you are thinking: But what if they say something that is completely ridiculous? Try this response:

"That is an interesting way of looking at that. I have never thought of it that way. Thanks for sharing your perspective."

This communicates that you heard them without necessarily agreeing with them. Then be curious. Ask for clarification. Ask how they came to this particular conclusion. As I am writing this, I sense that I need to point out the distinction between building connection and coaching/empowerment. I am offering these ideas as a means of building connection. The opportunity to coach will present itself eventually, but pivoting into offering advice or coaching as soon as you hear something "ridiculous" will most likely be viewed as just further evidence that you don't appreciate who they are or what they are going through, therefore damaging the connection. I bring this up because the effectiveness of your coaching is directly related to the quality of the connection you have with your teen at any given time.

I should also note that there will be times when your curiosity will be ignored or met with short answers. If you continue to probe when this happens, your teen will view this as intrusive or nosy. If you let it go when you teen clearly doesn't want to talk, you will be building a foundation for future conversations. Here is what this sounds like:

Your teen gets home from school and you say, "Anything interesting happen at school today?"

Your teen responds, "Not really."

You give it one more try. "How did the math test go?"

73

Teen: "Fine."

At this point you recognize they are not interested in talking right now so you wrap it up with something positive. "Well, I love you... Dinner will be in a bit."

There will be other times when they will open up to you. Especially if you ask about something they are interested in. Being curious without judgment can be very powerful. Here is what this can sound like:

One afternoon, my son Jimmy was playing a video game so I started with the obvious question: "What are you playing?"

He responded, "FIFA World Cup."

I asked, "Which team are you?"

Jimmy said, "The yellow team. Brazil."

I continued, "Are you just controlling one guy?"

At this point, he launched into an explanation of all of the buttons on the controller as well as some of the strategies involved.

So I took a leap of faith and asked, "Can I play?"

He didn't say it out loud, but I could tell he was thinking— fresh meat. He set up the game for two players and handed me a controller. Over the next 15 minutes, I continued to ask a lot of questions and he taught me how to play. Or maybe a better description is that he clearly demonstrated that he was the master and I was the student.

You will notice that many times when you are building connection with your teen, more than one of the strategies will come into play. In this case, curiosity led to the opportunity to be vulnerable and playful.

"Be curious, not judgmental."

—Walt Whitman

Being grateful:

Gratitude is experienced when you look for the good in others or what is working in your life. By placing your focus on what is good in your teenager and focusing on their strengths and talents, you will be not only helping them to develop a positive self image, you will also be helping these attributes to grow. Are you familiar with the law of attraction? The idea is that what you focus your attention on will grow. One distinction I would like to point out here is the difference between expressing gratitude for an action and expressing gratitude for an attribute. Here is a simple example of what I mean:

You come home from work and you notice that your teenager has taken the trash out. The first level of gratitude would be to thank them for taking the trash out.

You say, "I really appreciate you taking the trash out today." This is an example of expressing gratitude for an action.

The alternative is to thank them for their action while also acknowledging an attribute. You say, "Thanks for taking the trash out. I really appreciate your commitment to serving others and helping out around the house."

Remember the hero's two journeys. While you are empowering your teen to accomplish a variety of outside goals and tasks, you also have an opportunity to guide them on their journey toward building a loving character and being a *successful person*. Expressing gratitude for attributes as well as actions will go a long way in building connection with your teenager.

I would encourage you to consider two additional opportunities to build connection with your teen via gratitude. First, model gratitude by the way you engage with others and the way you live your life. Second, focus on becoming more grateful yourself. By focusing your attention on gratitude in all areas of your life, you will be setting an example for your teen as well as experiencing more peace, joy, and love. You will be moving both your teen and yourself toward our definition of a *successful person*.

There are an unlimited number of opportunities to express gratitude, such as being grateful for the service you receive at a restaurant, the grocery store, the movie theater, or anywhere else you are a customer. Then you can move on to others who have helped you throughout your life. Teachers, mentors, coaches, grandparents, and, of course, don't forget your own parents. Finally, there are the intangible aspects of your life. A beautiful sunrise or sunset. The joy of spending time with good friends. The way it feels to laugh at something that is really funny. The smell of a cup of coffee. You get the idea. Expressing gratitude is very attractive, and your teenager will be drawn in. They will enjoy being around you.

Now, there is one other area I would like to emphasize during this discussion of gratitude. Not only is this an opportunity to dramatically impact your life, it will have a huge impact on your teen. I am talking about experiencing and expressing gratitude for your spouse or partner. In a great number of the families I have worked with, the relationship between partners deteriorates when children come into the picture. Understandably, children require a lot of time and energy. Consequently, the original relationship that created the family becomes a second or third priority. The connection between partners can break down and become a source of pain if there is not some effort to develop it. Remember, what you put your attention on will grow, so it makes sense that what you don't pay attention to will stop growing and eventually start breaking down. When it comes to gratitude in your relationship, it is as simple as focusing on what brought you together in the first place—the attributes, traits, values, dreams, and beliefs that created the bond. What you fell in love with. Putting this into practice in everyday life can be a challenge, right? Work, carpool, cutting the grass, and a million other tasks require your attention. But I would ask, are any of these more important than the quality of your relationship with your partner? This relationship can be a tremendous source of joy or a tremendous source of pain. I would be remiss if I didn't mention that forgiveness plays an equally important role in the quality of the connection between partners. Forgiveness and gratitude are a dynamic duo that can literally transform your relationship.

So how does this impact your teen? While in the context of your relationship, you are partners. To your teen, you are their parents. When parents are good to each other, not only are you modeling what a healthy relationship looks like, you are providing much needed stability for your teen to lean on.

Additional Note:

Divorce is a reality for many families. If you find yourself reading this after a divorce, I am going to encourage you to open your heart to forgiving your former spouse and, yes, even putting your attention on what you are grateful for. Forgiveness and gratitude are the only ways to move past the pain and to regain peace, joy, and love in your life. Forgiveness and gratitude after a broken relationship are gifts to your children as well. Not only will they provide a path for peace, joy, and love to return to your life, forgiveness and gratitude will bring peace, joy, and love back into the home where your children live.

"Acknowledging the good that you already have in your life is the foundation for all abundance."

—Eckhart Tolle

Being kind:

Would you agree with the statement that there is not enough kindness in the world? For some people, acts of kindness are rarely experienced. So much so that it is hard to accept them. On the other hand, there are opportunities to offer acts of kindness all around us. Holding a door for someone and saying good morning. Offering your seat to someone on a crowded bus or subway. Picking up trash on the sidewalk.

For you teenager, pay attention to what they respond too. A good framework for kindness are the five love languages identified by Gary Chapman in his book *The Five Love Languages of Teenagers*.

- Words of affirmation
- Physical touch
- Quality time
- Acts of service
- Gifts

Here is an example for each of these:

Words of affirmation:

- Saying, "I love you"
- Saying, "I believe in you"
- Saying, "You can do this"
- Acknowledging traits or attributes like compassion, kindness, work ethic, generosity, etc.

Physical touch:

- For your daughter, combine physical touch with an act of service. Offer to paint her fingernails and toenails.
- For your son, get in the habit of sharing a fist bump or high-five as a greeting or when he is coming or going.
- Hang on to the habit of a hug or kiss on the cheek.

Quality time:

- Sit with them and just listen.
- Play a card game or board game.
- Invite them to come help you pick out a major purchase: new car, kitchen table, computer, or phone.

Acts of service:

- Cook their favorite meal for dinner
- Offer to drive them and their friends somewhere.
- Help with hair or makeup before a dance.
- Help wash the car before a date.

Gifts:

- Take their car and put $20 worth of gas in it.
- Buy movie tickets for them and their friends

- Treat them and their friends to ice cream, boba tea, or coffee.

A word of caution is appropriate here. There is a difference between an act of kindness and enabling or rescuing your teenager.

For example: Your teenager is studying for a test after dinner and they realize that they left one of the books they need at school. Offering to go to the school, the library, or a friend's house and pick up a copy for them could be viewed as an act of kindness. However, if you rescue them in this situation, you may be missing out on an opportunity to coach and empower them to solve problems and be more responsible. This is an example of a circumstance in which there is not a clear-cut answer for what to do. The current state of your relationship, previous conversations and expectations, and your intuition are all factors that could impact what you do. Remember that you are on a journey as well. A journey to always respond with love, to master the art of building connections and empowering others. I can guarantee you that there will be times when you will look back and think, I could have handled that differently. When this happens, forgive yourself and focus your attention on what you have learned, how you have grown, and your commitment to build a *successful family*. My wife likes to say: Give yourself grace.

As we wrap up this conversation on building the connection with your teenager, consider these coaching questions:

- In terms of your connection with your teenager, what would be a breakthrough over the next few weeks or few months?

Building on prior success:

- Of the strategies discussed in this chapter for building connection, which ones have you naturally used in the past?
- How has this worked for you?
- How could you build on this success?

Stretching yourself:

- Of these strategies, which ones sound like something that would be uncomfortable?
- How else could you look at that particular strategy?
- What are you willing to try in the next 24 hours?
- What would stop you from doing this in the next 24 hours?

Section 3: Ten Coaching Skills to Empowering Your Teenager to Be Their Absolute Best

If empowerment and character development are the goals, then empowerment coaching is the process. So what is empowerment coaching and how is it different from teaching, offering advice, or mentoring? The empowerment coach understands the value of two particular elements of personal development. First, the empowerment coach believes that the person being coached is the most qualified to design the solution for their particular goals or issues. This is because the person being coached is the expert in their own life. Therefore, the coach's role is to guide people being coached to look within themselves for answers. To trust their intuition. Second, the empowerment coach understands the value of experiential learning. The coach supports and encourages those being coached as they work their plans and take action. Through the process of taking action, valuable experience and wisdom are gained. In fact, the only path to transformation is through personal experience.

A simple example of experiential learning is the process of learning to ride a bike. You can know everything about riding a bike. You can be able to pass a test on the techniques involved and know the theory of balance and still not be able to actually ride a bike. The only way to "get" riding a bike is to get on the bike and try to ride it. It is through action that personal development and transformation happen.

Therefore, the empowerment coach resists the urge to provide answers or to pass judgment on the solutions of the person being coached. The coach's primary role is to use open-ended questions to help the person being coached to flesh out what is the next step for them, see what is holding them back, and figure out how they can use what they have learned.

As a parent, there will be times where it will be appropriate to teach or mentor your teenager. However, the greatest gift you can give your teenager is to develop and put into practice the skills of an empowerment coach.

Think of it this way. While it is important to teach your teenager skills like driving, mathematics, or doing their own laundry, once they have learned these skills your role shifts to one of empowerment. Empowering them to use what they have learned in their pursuit of being a *successful person*.

It is important to point out the difference between empowerment coaching, teaching, and offering advice. As parents of teenagers, we naturally gravitate toward the role of teacher or one who is offering advice. What we miss is that in many cases we have taught a particular lesson many times. In fact, we get frustrated because our child is still making the same mistakes even after we have shared our wisdom. This frustration is a signal that it is time to move to the role of an empowerment coach. Your teenager knows what to do, they just haven't internalized the lesson through their own personal experiences. Unfortunately, the skills of empowerment coaching are not as familiar and don't come as naturally as the skills of a teacher or advisor. Which sounds easier to you: talking and telling our teen what we think they should do or listening without judgment and without offering solutions? It is difficult but necessary to point your teenager to their own intuition and let them develop their own solutions. To let your teenager experience the consequences of their actions and decisions because you know that valuable wisdom is gained through personal experience.

I may be a little ahead of myself here. There is another role that we as parents must relinquish before we can even be willing to explore the possibilities of empowerment coaching. We have to let go of our need to control what our teenager is doing. When children are young it is appropriate for parents to exercise some control over the life of the child. As children move into their teenage years, the control of their lives should naturally transition from the parent to the teen. After all, the end goal is to prepare your child to go out into the world as an able adult. I have noticed that parents have a tendency to underestimate their child's ability to manage or control their own lives, while at the same time the teenager will many times overestimate their readiness to manage and control their own lives. Therein lies the biggest source of pain for the parent/teen relationship. It is important to note that this is why building a strong connection with your teenager is so important. The stronger the connection, the more insight you will have into your teenager's readiness.

Coaching Skills:

We are going to explore ten coaching skills that you can put into practice with your teenager. These skills are the foundation for being a source of empowerment.

1. Clarifying
2. Acknowledging
3. Validating
4. Reframing
5. Identifying limiting beliefs
6. Visioning
7. Designing a plan
8. Being accountable
9. Celebrating
10. Inspiring

Before we dive into these coaching skills let's take a high-level look at the coaching process.

There are four basic steps for you to use:

1. Connecting
2. Call to action
3. Shifting Perspective and Mindset
4. Reconnecting

Connecting:

Connecting is the process of clearly identifying where your teenager is at the present time. The goal is to bring to the surface the current set of circumstances and their current state of mind. Keep in mind that in order for them to move forward, any negative emotional energy will need to be allowed to dissipate. The coaching skills used here are clarifying, acknowledging, and validating.

Call to Action:

Once the current state of mind and circumstances have been established, it is time to design the plan to move forward. This is where visioning comes into play. First, the goal is to determine what would be ideal. Next, you will help your teenager design their own action plan. The obvious coaching skills here are visioning and designing a plan.

Note: There will be times when your teenager will get stuck during the call to action step. When this happens, move to the reframing skills to create a sense of hope. Also, if you notice them getting emotional, circle back to connecting to allow them to feel safe and give them the needed time to let the negative emotional energy dissipate.

Shifting Perspective and Mindset:

The purpose of shifting perspective and mindset is to move your teenager past any obstacles they see. This is accomplished by challenging them to see the circumstances differently. To take a different perspective. The coaching skills used here are identifying limiting beliefs and reframing.

Reconnecting:

Reconnecting is the process of checking in to see how the action plan worked out and how your teenager is doing. This happens hours, days, or even weeks after the first conversation. The first coaching skill used in this step is being accountable. This is simply checking in to see what has happened. This is first because depending on how their plan worked out there are two different ways to follow up.

If the plan works out great, we next celebrate their accomplishment and inspire them toward the future.

If the plan doesn't work, we go back to the first coaching skills, using acknowledging, clarifying, and validating.

Please note that while I have presented the coaching process as four steps, in practice it is a fluid process. You will find yourself jumping between steps. It may be helpful to think of each of these steps as a service you can provide to your teenager. Your role is to stay present so that you can identify what your teenager needs at the moment and then provide the appropriate "service."

- When you notice that they are stuck, you move to shifting perspective and mindset.
- If they start to move into a fearful or negative emotional state, you move to reconnecting.
- Once they have recovered, you return to shifting perspective and mindset.
- As they begin to see hope for the future, you move to a call to action.
- If they get stuck on something, you move back to shifting perspective and mindset.

Can you see why I say it is a fluid process? Developing your ability to recognize what is needed at the moment and offer the appropriate "service" is a beautiful gift you can give to your teenager.

Your teen is going to have a lot of outer goals where your coaching will come into play. Outer goals could include everything from getting a good grade on a test to picking out an outfit for the first day of school to getting a summer job to learning how to drive. As you coach and empower them to accomplish these outer goals, however, don't forget about the second journey they are on. The journey to become a *successful person*. This is a journey to a loving character. I invite you to consider this:

While accomplishing their outside goals will seem like life or death to your teenager, to the empowerment-centered parent, your teenager's outside goals are just the vehicle used to instill love-based principles, values, and beliefs. The development of a loving character is always the first priority.

Let's take a more-detailed look at the ten coaching skills one by one.

Clarifying: Have you noticed that your teenager will use words in ways that don't make sense to you? There has always been a special language for the hip and cool life of a teenager. It was that way when you were a teen, so why would it be different now? Clarifying is the process of helping your teenager think things through and clearly identify what it is that they are saying. At the same time, this process helps the parent get clear on what the teen is trying to say.

Here are some clarifying questions:

- What do you mean when you say…?
- I am not sure if I know what you mean when you use that word What would I say instead?
- Tell me more about…

Example:

Teenager: I don't know if I can deal with Jane anymore… She is just so extra.
Parent: What do you mean by extra?
Teenager: She is just no fun because everything has to be her way.
Parent: So being extra is being bossy?
Teenager: No. It is not just being bossy. Like today. She got all worked up because there were some other kids sitting

at the lunch table we normally sit at and she just wouldn't let it go. You know, extra.
Parent: So I might say being over the top or being ridiculous. Does that sound right?
Teenager: Yeah.

Acknowledging: This is the process of letting your teenager know that you really listened to what they said. All of us have a desire to feel like we have been heard. Acknowledging is accomplished by paraphrasing or repeating back what your teenager has said.

Here are some ways to approach acknowledging:

- What you are saying is...
- Let me see if I get this...
- I am hearing you say...
- What you are telling me is...
- Let me say it back to you, just to make sure I got it.

Example:

Teenager: I am really trying to do better in math, but my grade isn't getting any better.
Parent: I am hearing you say that you are putting forth more effort in math but you are not seeing the results you had hoped for.

Validating: The goal of validating is to let your teenager know that they have the right to feel the way they do while at the same time not passing judgment on those feelings. You are not saying that their feelings are right or wrong. Just that you can see the circumstance from their perspective. Validating is a close cousin to acknowledging. Acknowledging is focused on what was said, while validating is focused on feelings:

What validating sounds like:

- I can see how that would make you angry.
- Based on your values, no wonder you feel the way you do.
- That is perfectly normal. It can be very upsetting when something like that happens.
- Given what you have been through, it doesn't surprise me that you feel that way.

Example:

Teenager: I am so mad about getting a B- on my chemistry final.
Parent: Given how hard you studied, it makes sense that you feel that way.

Reframing: The goal of reframing is to see a particular circumstance from a different perspective. Typically, when your teenager feels stuck or hopeless, they are seeing their circumstance from a fearful perspective. The reframing process points them back to their love-based principles, values, and beliefs so that they can shift to a loving perspective. Most of the time, this process just involves asking reframing questions that point your teen in a new direction. However, if they are really struggling, you may need to share an alternative way of looking at the circumstance.

Reframing questions:

- How else could you look at this?
- (if your teen is having an interpersonal problem) If you look at it from the other person's perspective, what do you think they are feeling?
- How could this be a good thing?

- What are you grateful for?
- What did you learn about yourself?

Example:

Teenager: I am never going to be able to pass my economics test this Friday.
Parent: You did okay on the last test. What study strategies did you use then?
Teenager: The problem is that this chapter is a lot harder.
Parent: Oh, I see. But how could taking a hard class like this be a good thing for you?
Teenager: It isn't.

If your teenager gets stuck, you may need to offer an alternative perspective on the heels of the previous discussion:.

Parent: Would it be okay if I share another way of looking at this?
Teenager: Yeah, I guess.
Parent: My guess is that the rest of this year and when you go to college your classes are not going to be getting easier. So maybe you could look at this economics class as a chance to learn some new study habits. You are a smart kid; once you figure out the best way for you to prepare for a class like this, it will make the rest of the hard classes you take a lot easier for you.

Identifying limiting beliefs: Sometimes your teenager will get stuck. They will not be able to see a way past their current circumstances. Identifying limiting beliefs comes into play when your efforts to reframe aren't effective in creating a sense of hope. Think of this process as identifying and reframing a core principle, value, or belief.

This is fundamental to shifting from a fearful perspective to a loving perspective.

Questions for identifying limiting beliefs:

- What is stopping you from moving forward?
- What is holding you back?
- What part of you is talking right now?
- What are you afraid of?
- How is that working out for you?

Example:

Teenager: Eighth grade has been really hard. I don't know how I am going to be able to survive high school.
Parent: What are you most afraid of?
Teenager: The high school is so much bigger. How am I going to find my way around? What if I never see any of my friends anymore?
Parent: Sounds like you are not sure if you are ready for high school.
Teenager: Yeah.

Visioning: Visioning is the process of exploring what it possible and what would be an ideal outcome. I could just as easily have called this process goal setting, but I wanted to encompass the idea of stretch goals as well. Sure, we can set everyday goals, but there is value in also stretching past our limiting beliefs. It should be noted that there is something different about saying our goals and stretch goals out loud. Having your teenager tell you their goals makes them real. It brings additional energy and commitment to them.

Visioning questions:

- What would be ideal?
- In a perfect world, what would you like to see happen?

- If money wasn't an issue, what would you do?
- If time wasn't an issue, what would you do?
- Last year you raised $5,000 during the marching band car wash. What about setting a goal of $10,000 for this year?

Example:

Teenager: I am thinking about running for a class officer position.
Parent: That is awesome. In a perfect world, what position would you like to have?
Teenager: Mike is going to run for president. It would be really cool if I could be vice president. Together we could make a big difference.
Parent: That's exciting. What is the first thing you would do?
Teenager: We have talked about getting a "real" DJ for the homecoming dance. Nothing against Mr. Jones, but the only reason they asked him to do it last year was because he is a teacher and he did it for free.

Designing a plan: This is the process of creating the action plan to achieve the stated goal. Depending on the scope or size of the goal, this could entail only one or two steps or it could be multiple steps to be carried out over an extended period of time. The role of the coach/parent is to support and guide your teenager through the process of laying out a plan. This is another area where it is important to resist the temptation to provide the answers or offer unsolicited advice. It is their plan and they will be more invested in executing the plan when they own it.

Questions for designing a plan:

- What do you need to do first?
- How long is that going to take?

- What are you willing to commit to doing this week?
- What will need to happen next?

Example:

Parent: So the goal is to get an A on your math test next week. What are you going to do this week to get ready?
Teenager: I am going to get up early on Wednesday and Friday and go to the study group the teacher has before school.
Parent: That sounds like a great idea. How are you going to get there? Do you need me to take you?
Teenager: If you could take Beth and me on Wednesday, Beth's mom will take us on Friday.
Parent: Sounds good. What else are you going to do?
Teenager: I am going to spend one hour each night this week doing practice problems. Then Beth and I are going to meet at Starbucks on Saturday morning to study together.
Parent: Sounds like a good plan.

Being accountable: The goal of accountability is to help your teenager keep the commitments they have made. It is important to note that this is not about blaming them or making them feel guilty. It is about helping them identify a measurable result and the time frame they are willing to commit to. If for some reason the goal is not achieved, you acknowledge the facts and move to lessons learned through the process of trying.

Accountability questions:

- How will we both know that you have done what you said you will do?
- How are you going to measure your progress?
- By what date are you hoping to accomplish this goal?

- Would it help if I checked in with you to see how you are doing?

Continuing the math test example from the call to action section:

Parent: How are you going to measure your progress?
Teenager: I have added the morning study group and the one-hour study session each night to my calendar. I am planning to mark them off as I complete them.
Parent: Would it help if I checked in with you to see how you are doing?
Teenager: I should be good during the week. Let's see how I am doing after Beth and I study on Saturday morning.

Celebrating: Just like it sounds, this is the process of celebrating your teenager's accomplishments and growth. Celebrating can also involve believing in your teen even when they don't. It is awesome to accomplish a goal, but it is even better to be able to share the experience with someone who is fully aware of all that was overcome in the process.

What celebrating sounds like:

- Congratulations on the A on your math test! I bet it feels really good to know that your hard work paid off.
- I know you were really nervous about auditioning for that part in the school play but you did it!
- Congratulations on getting your driver's license! Where are you going to go first?

Example:

Teenager: Can you believe that we won that game? The other team was ranked #3 in the state.
Parent: I know. You have to be really proud of yourself and

your teammates for sticking together even when you were behind. What happened that turned it around?

Teenager: A couple of the seniors really got us fired up in the 4th quarter.

Parent: Wow. It was really a special night. You are going to remember this forever.

Inspiring: Inspiring is the process of seeing and acknowledging the strengths and abilities of your teenager. Even when they don't. This is similar to the building connection skill of being a source of hope. The intention is to see the absolute best in your teenager. To focus their attention on the attributes they have that put them in the position to accomplish their goals.

What inspiring your teenager sounds like:

- You have an amazing ability to make people feel welcome and important. It makes a big difference to your friends.
- You have a great sense of humor. Thanks for making me and your brother laugh so much.
- I really appreciate your commitment to doing well in school. Your work ethic is going to serve you well throughout your life.
- I have noticed that you are really good at solving problems. You think really logically.

Example:

Teenager: I have so much homework to do this weekend. I am never going to get all of this done.

Parent: (acknowledging) Sounds like you are feeling a little overwhelmed.

Teenager: Yeah, I wish my teachers didn't think that their class was the only one I am taking.

Parent: That would be nice, wouldn't it?

Teenager: (Smiles) Yeah.

Parent: (inspiring) One thing I know about you is that you are really good at organizing your thoughts and making a plan. It is like a superpower that you have.

Teenager: Thanks... Well, I'd better get started.

So these are the ten fundamental skills for empowerment coaching. Hopefully you are starting to see how these skills could be combined with the skills for building connections to transform your relationship with your teenager. Before we move on to putting it all into practice, here are a few more thoughts on the process of empowerment coaching.

Being the parent of a teenager is a journey:

You should know right now that you will never have it all figured out, and that is okay. This is because the family dynamic is in a constant state of change. There will always be the next set of circumstances. Consider how these changes might affect your family dynamics and the relationship with your teenager:

- Your teenager gets their driver's license.
- One of you teenager's best friends moves to a new city.
- Your teenager gets the lead in the school play.
- Your teenager doesn't get the lead in the school play.
- You get a new job that requires you to move the family to a new city.
- Your oldest child goes to college, leaving two siblings behind.
- Your teenager and a group of their friends get caught drinking and are suspended from school for three days.

The point is that there will always be new challenges. New opportunities for us to learn and grow as parents. You need to be okay with the fact that there will be times when you won't know what to do or you may do something that seems to make things worse. This is all part of the journey to becoming a better parent and a better person.

As a parent interested in empowering your teenager, you have to trust that they have the ability to find their own answers:

One of the biggest challenges we face as our child moves into their teenage years is resisting the urge to provide all of the answers and control everything. I have found it helpful to shift my focus from the immediate issue or challenge to the long-term goal of developing my teenager's problem-solving skills and the make-up of their character. Remember that the goal is for them to be able to go out into the world and be a "successful" person. This starts by them taking ownership of their choices and the corresponding consequences. When we focus on empowerment, we appreciate the power of experiential learning. We understand that the process of our teenager finding their own answers is much more impactful than us telling them what to do or, worse, us doing it for them.

Learning and wisdom are cumulative for both the parent and the teenager:

Think about a little boy learning to count. Counting is in the world of mathematics, but until the child masters counting, he cannot even conceive of the possibility of addition or subtraction. Furthermore, to even begin talking with the child about multiplication or division, he will have to have mastered the fundamentals of addition and subtraction.

This same process applies when we are talking about the values found in a loving character. Consider this: Is it possible that there are ways to look at respect, compassion, gratitude, or forgiveness that we cannot recognize today? Experience has taught me that, indeed, there are. Learning is a cumulative, lifelong process.

Part 4: Putting It All into Practice

In this final section, we are going to explore how choosing empowerment over control—choosing love over fear—looks in everyday life when parenting a teenager. Below you will find 19 scenarios. Obviously, every family dynamic is different and there are endless potential variations to these stories. The intention is to create a picture in your mind of how these strategies can play out in the typical circumstances you face every day. Take time to envision how you would phrase a question or how you would shift from a fearful mindset to a loving mindset. Most importantly, remember to let go of your need to "do it right." Focus on being present, building connections, and empowering your teenager to be their absolute best. Parenting a teenager is a journey. Every day, you and your teenager will face new challenges and changing circumstances. This is exactly what is supposed to happen. If you open up to the possibility of love, it is in these everyday moments that your family will be transformed.

It seems appropriate to note here that there may be times where you should seek professional help. If you experience a steady deterioration of a situation over two or three months or a dramatic change in your teenager's mood or behavior, find a counselor that can do an assessment of your teen. This is critical if you suspect substance abuse or any other self-destructive behaviors. While the strategies and techniques I have presented in this book are great for improving or reversing a negative trend within your home, the outside perspective of a professional counselor could be the key to healing a teenager who is struggling with big issues.

We'll now work through these 19 scenarios and ideas:

1. Manners and disrespect
2. Laziness and not taking responsibility
3. "Come out of your room and talk to the rest of the family!"
4. "I just caught my 15-year-old son vaping... What should I do?"
5. "How do I get my child to try harder in school?"
6. Trouble with friends
7. Concerns over choice of friends
8. Making bad choices on Saturday night
9. When to say no vs. when to say yes
10. "How do I get my teenager to talk to me?"
11. The number one thing your teenager wishes you would do better
12. Big talks: Drugs, alcohol, sex
13. Disrupting the family
14. Breaking curfew
15. The power of a hand-written note
16. Conflict: Crossing your teen's will
17. If you are willing to listen, your teen will provide valuable feedback for your growth as a parent.
18. Empowering your teenager to overcome mean-spirited comments
19. Why your teenager needs to make mistakes

Manners and disrespect:

Question from a parent:

My 13-year-old seems to have forgotten any manners. No "thank you" when someone drops her off, or "please" at a restaurant or anything. Any ideas?

Having manners, being kind, and behaving in a respectful way are fundamental elements of a loving character. In this scenario, the teenager seems to have "forgotten" her manners, which implies that these lessons have already been taught.

There are two possibilities here. First, they are simply distracted by everything that it is to be a teenager. So my initial thought is to remind them about the importance of manners in a respectful and compassionate way.

First, remind them through your own actions. Take an honest look at how you are modeling kindness and manners. In this situation, it may be helpful to emphasize your gratitude, especially with your teenager. For example: While at dinner, say to your teen. "Sarah, could you please pass the salt?" When she does, emphasize the "thank you," saying, "Thank you, I really appreciate that." This may seem a little basic, but sometimes the best way to regain your form is to focus on the fundamentals.

Second, offer a simple verbal reminder at the appropriate time. For example: When your teenager gets home from school you make them a snack to eat while they are doing their homework. As you set the snack down, if there is no acknowledgment or thank you, you simply say, "Manners…" The key here is to be mindful of your mindset. If you are coming from a place of disappointment or anger, your teenager will pick up on this. They will feel attacked and like you are trying to control them; consequently they will put up their defenses. Which is exactly what you would do if someone did this to you. Instead, reframe their lack of response from a perspective of compassion and forgiveness. Now, when you say "Manners…," it will be received as a loving reminder of their childhood lessons about kindness and respect. I can't emphasize enough how important your mindset is here. It is not what you say. It is all about how you say it.

Now, it is quite possible that your teenager will not respond to your compassionate reminder. If this is the case, I would suggest that through this "bad behavior" they are calling out to you. They are calling for your love and to reconnect. Something is going on that has them feeling isolated, overwhelmed, or uncertain. Maybe something has happened within their friend group. Maybe they are overwhelmed by the newness of the start of a new school year. Maybe they are struggling with one or more of their classes. The point is that this is not about the lack of manners. The lack of manners is a symptom or a signal that they need to level up their connection with you. Start with a compassionate check-in on how they are doing. Something like this:

"Sarah, you seem like you have been a little off lately. I can only imagine how overwhelming being a freshman is. The high school is so much bigger and the classes have got to be harder. Is there anything you would like to talk about? I promise to just listen."

If your teen doesn't open up at this point, you just need to continue to develop your connection. Once the connection is strong enough, they will either open up to you or they will resolve the issue on their own. In either case, they will rediscover their own gratitude and the manners will return.

Laziness and not taking responsibility:

Question from a parent:

How can I help a teenage girl to stop being lazy and start taking responsibilities—like keeping her room neat, doing her laundry, and helping out in the kitchen?

There are a couple of different aspects to this question. In this case, I am going to focus on the issue of the teen keeping her room neat. The state of their bedroom frequently causes conflict between teenagers and their parents. But if we look at it from a coaching perspective, this challenge presents an opportunity for parents to transition from control to empowerment.

Before talking about her bedroom, take a moment to assess your state of mind. For this conversation to be effective, you need to be firmly grounded in a loving perspective. If you are experiencing any fear-based emotions like disappointment or anger, your first task is to reframe the circumstance. As always, the best place to start is with forgiveness, gratitude, and compassion.

Once you have regained a love-based state of mind, remind yourself that the goal is to empower your teenager to BE responsible. This can only be accomplished by relinquishing some of your control to them. Here is an example of what this conversation could sound like.

Parent: Amy, the state of your bedroom has turned into a source of conflict between us. I don't like it when we fight, so I have an idea I want to run by you. Someday, you are going to move out on your own and one of my goals is to do what I can to make sure you are ready for that day. When you get your own place, you will be responsible for taking care of it, so I was thinking that it makes sense for you to get some practice now. Here is what I am thinking. Your bedroom can be your practice space. If you feel like you are ready for it, from now on, you will be in charge of your room and the stuff in it. Do you feel like you are ready to take this on?

Amy: Yeah. That is what I have been saying.

Parent: I do have a couple of conditions that we need to agree to. First, if the way you are managing your room has an impact on the rest of us in the house, you agree to work out a solution that works for all of us.

Amy: What do you mean?

Parent: Here is an example of how you could impact the rest of the house. What if we are having a family dinner and there aren't enough plates because they all are in your room? Can you see how this could be an issue?

Amy: Yeah, but that will never happen.

Parent: Probably not, but you see what I am talking about. There are two other conditions. Nothing illegal can happen in your room and no boys in your room. Does this sound fair to you?

Amy: I can live with that.

Parent: So, you are in charge of your room and your stuff. You are ready to take responsibility for what goes on in your room. This is a big step so I just want to make sure you're ready.

Amy: Yeah, I got this.

With this conversation, you have set the stage for future teaching/empowerment opportunities. Turn over the responsibility and the consequences to your teen. When they come to you with an issue related to their choices or decisions, resist the urge to rescue them. Compassionately, let them experience the full weight of the consequences of their actions and coach them through the process of solving the problem on their own.

For example: When they come to you and complain that they have nothing to wear to school because all of their clothes are dirty, you respond compassionately: "That is a bummer. What are you going to do?" You can talk about what it means to be responsible and make good decisions all day long without any impact. But it is in a moment like this when your teenager will actually get it.

"Come out of your room and talk to the rest of the family!":

Question from a parent:

What do you do when your teenager hardly ever comes out of their room, and when they do come out they don't talk or engage with the family in any way?

In this scenario, making your teenager come out of their room and demanding that they join in with the family will only serve to damage the connection your teenager feels with you and the family. I recommend working to build the connection with your teenager so that they want to join you. So that they appreciate and enjoy the time with the family. I have to acknowledge that this can be a challenge and may take some time, but it is possible. In fact, I would assert that your teenager deep down inside wants this connection.

So what do you do to develop your connection? First, take an honest look at the environment within your home. I realize that all families have conflict and issues to deal with, but the more peace, joy, warmth, and love within your home, the more attractive the environment will be to your teenager. The more connected they will feel. This is where your own personal development comes into play. Are you being intentional about choosing love and empowerment as the way you engage with all the people in your house? Are you being a source of peace, joy, warmth, and love within your home? If after some self-reflection, you determine that you could do better, awesome. Awareness is always the first step in transformation.

Now here is an interesting twist to your commitment to personal development. One of the ways to develop connection with your teenager is by being vulnerable. In this scenario, you could have this conversation with your teen.

Parent: Nick, can we talk for a minute?

Nick: I am kind of busy, can it wait?

Parent: This will only take a few minutes. I wanted to apologize for a couple of things.

Nick: (at this point feeling a little curious) Sure. I guess.

Parent: I feel like I could be doing a better job of creating a happy home for you to come home to. When I take a minute to think about it, I realize that being a teenager can be super exciting but at the same time can be tough. Between your school work, friends, and thinking about what you want to do after high school, there is a lot going on for you. What occurred to me is that with all of the stress in your life, it could be really helpful if our house could be a source of peace, joy, and love for you. Now we do okay, but I feel like I could do better. So I wanted to let you know that I am going to work on being more forgiving and compassionate. I also want to find some ways to empower you and help you get ready for the day when you move out on your own.

How do you think your teenager would respond to a conversation like this? The key is that you are not blaming them or making them wrong for their behavior.

See if this rings true for you. In most situations in your life, you will resist being controlled but will welcome empowerment. This is no different for your teenager.

"I just caught my 15-year-old son vaping... What should I do?"

If you are facing a situation like this, it makes sense that you are concerned or worried about the choices your teenager is making and the potential impact on their health. That being said, trying to control what they do through demands and punishments is only going to damage your relationship and cause conflict.

Your teenager will soon be an adult. They will be responsible for making their own decisions and taking ownership of their results and consequences. In a case like this, the alternative to trying to control what they do is to inspire them to make informed and educated decisions.

A first step would be to look for ways to deepen your connection with your teenager. This is important because the level of influence you have with your child is directly related to the quality of your connection with them. Without a great connection, you will have little chance to influence the choices they make. There are an endless number of ways to build your connection with your teenager. Take a car ride together, play a card game, ask them for help with something they are good at, acknowledge a trait you appreciate about them. As the connection deepens your influence will grow.

Then when you print off an article on the health risks of vaping and leave it on their bed, they will take the time to read it.

Then when you ask them if they have considered the health risk, they won't get defensive.

Then when you suggest they resist peer pressure and make decisions based on what is best for them, they will appreciate your perspective.

As an extension of these conversations about the health risk, there may be potential consequences at their school or legal issues. Consider bringing these issues up from an empowerment perspective. For example:

Parent: (acknowledging what happened) We both know I saw you vaping the other day. What happens at school if you get caught?

Teenager: I'm not going to get caught.

Parent: Maybe not, but wouldn't it make sense to know what could happen if somehow you did get caught? Where could you look to see if there are any rules against it at school?

Teenager: I don't see why it matters... I'm not stupid enough to get caught.

Parent: I hear you, and maybe there aren't any big consequences at school, but what if there are? For example: What if the rule is that you can't graduate if you get caught vaping? Wouldn't it make sense to at least know what could happen...just in case? I mean...what would you do if you couldn't graduate?

With this approach you are empowering them to take responsibility for their choices, while at the same time you are teaching them to be more thoughtful. Again, keep in mind that a conversation like this is just one block in the foundation you are trying to build. Continue to deepen your connection and look for creative ways to share your values. The ultimate goal is to empower them to be their absolute best, including taking care of their own health and well-being.

"How do I get my teenager to try harder in school?"

Declining or poor grades can become a source of conflict during the high school years. Especially if your teenager has always been a good student. Let's say that up until eighth or ninth grade your son or daughter always was eager to go to school. They focused on their homework and breezed through tests. But now things have changed. Now, you never see them studying and when you ask how they are doing in their classes, you get the classic response: Fine. Then the report card comes home and instead of the usual A's and B's there are C's, D's, and even a F. Can we agree that in this situation, life is putting the squeeze on you?

As with all of our parenting challenges, we have an opportunity to choose how we will respond. For now, I am going to focus on the circumstance of seeing the report card and the initial discussion with your child.

If this has happened to you, think back to the moment when you were opening the report card and seeing the declining grades. If this hasn't happened, put yourself in this situation. What did you experience (or what do you imagine you would experience)?

For most of us, the initial experience is going to be a combination of disappointment, anger, and frustration. As we have discussed before, these emotions are reflective of a fear-based perspective and in a moment like this it is natural for us to be pulled into a fearful perspective.

So what happens next? This is one of the many moments of truth we face every day in which we have the opportunity to choose between control and empowerment. Between fear and love.

If you respond or engage out of your frustration or anger, there will be conflict. You will demand that your teenager share all of their homework assignments with you so you can check their work. You will inform them that they will not be able to go out with their friends on the weekends until there has been an improvement in their grades. Your teenager will either yell at you, saying things a teenager should never say to their parents, or they will sit nonresponsive with their arms folded. Does this sound familiar or seem realistic?

Or you can create a pause. A pause gives the opportunity for you to make a choice. You can ask yourself the following: Do I want to engage from a fear-based control perspective or do I want to engage from a love-based empowerment perspective?

In order to make the shift to a love-based empowerment perspective, ask the following:

- What am I grateful for?
- What is my teenager going through or what does school look like from their perspective?
- What do I need to forgive them for?

Once you are grounded in gratitude, compassion, and forgiveness, you are in a position to ask the important question:

- How can I make a difference?

Once grounded in your intention to empower, you will see this situation differently. First, you will see this shift in behavior as a sign that your teenager is feeling isolated or disconnected. You may never be able to understand why or what happened, but you can always look for ways to deepen your connection with them. Secondly, from an empowerment perspective, you see that these are *their* grades. Your teenager is responsible for the results and the consequences. Your role is to support them along their journey. Here is an example of how the initial conversation might go:

Parent: (in a calm and compassionate way) I saw your report card. Obviously, I was surprised. To be honest, at this moment I am not as concerned about the grades as I am about how you're doing. It just seems out of character for you, so I want to make sure that you are okay. Are you feeling overwhelmed? Or are there issues with your friends?

Teenager: I'm fine. My classes are just stupid.

(Note: Your teenager will rarely open up on the first attempt, but know that they did hear your concern and they did appreciate your support.)

Parent: (in a forgiving and non-judgmental way) Okay. I want you to know that I am available to talk if you want and that I will try really hard to just listen and understand what you are going through. Also, now that you are in high school I know that these are *your* grades. Again, I am here to support you, but ultimately they are your responsibility. I am curious... What do you mean when you say your classes are stupid?

With this approach the parent has set the stage for their teenager to open up about any issues they are dealing with, while at the same time they have transferred responsibility for the grades to their teenager. They have made the transition from control to empowerment.

Trouble with friends:

A questions from a parent:

My daughter came home upset because one of her best friends from junior high has started hanging out with a different group of girls. What do I say to her?

If this hasn't happened to your child yet, it probably will at some point during junior high school, high school, or college.

113

One of their best friends from grade school or junior high will find a new interest or a new group of friends. In fact, if you think back to your childhood and high school years, I bet you can name a "best friend" that you drifted away from by the time you left your teenage years. This is a time of exploration and personal growth for all teenagers, so there are bound to be some friendships that get left behind in the pursuit of new interests and changing values.

Your first role in a situation like this is to rebuild connection with your daughter and provide a safe place for her to work through the emotions she is feeling. This is a perfect time to work on being compassionate. Think of it this way. Your daughter feels like she is losing a connection with a long-time friend. This is bound to stir up feelings of being isolated or alone. Your compassion will provide a much needed sense of connection. Here is how that might sound:

Teenager: I can't believe Beth sat with those girls from her drama club today at lunch. She looked right at me and then walked right past our table to theirs.

Parent: That sounds like it was really disappointing to you.

Teenager: I think I am more mad than disappointed. I mean we have been friends since fifth grade and I even went to the play her and her drama club friends were in, and now it is like I don't even exist.

Parent: I can tell that this was really upsetting to you. It can't even imagine what that must have been like.

At this point, listen to your intuition to determine if she is ready to talk more or if she needs some time to let the negative energy dissipate. If she seems ready to talk, you can shift to some empowerment coaching questions. If she doesn't seem ready, let some time pass. In a couple of days, you can ask how it is going with Beth. When she is ready, use your coaching skills to lead her to her own love-based solution. Here is what this could sound like:

Parent: One of the great things about being a human being is that we have the power to choose how we respond to situations like this. Are you interested in trying to heal your relationship with Beth?

Teenager: Yeah. I don't like feeling awkward and mad all of the time.

Parent: I have found that the first step in healing a relationship when something like this happens is to offer forgiveness. How do you think forgiveness could help in this situation?

Teenager: I might think about forgiving her if she would apologize about the way she has been treating me.

Parent: What if she never apologizes?

Teenager: Well, then I guess I would never forgive her.

Parent: How would that move you guys forward or make things better?

Teenager: It wouldn't...but I didn't do anything wrong. She is the one who doesn't seem to care about me and our other friends.

Parent: I can tell that this makes you sad. Maybe you could try to see it from her perspective... What is it about the drama club that she likes so much?

Teenager: Well, she is pretty good at it and even when we were younger she always talked about being in plays or on TV. I think it makes her feel like she is good at something.

Parent: That makes sense.
Teenager: I know that this is really cool for her, but I still miss hanging out with her.

Parent: If you listen to your heart, what do you feel like you should do?

Teenager: I know I shouldn't hold it against her. She is just following her dreams.

Parent: Maybe you should sleep on it. See how you feel in the morning. How does that sound?

Teenager: Yeah…that makes sense.

In the end, these relationships may or may not continue into adulthood for your teenager. But in either case, these situations provide a great opportunity for personal development. Our teenagers can deepen their appreciation of the choice between being fear based or love based and with this they will be well on their way to becoming a source of peace, joy, warmth, and love wherever they go.

Concerns over choice of friends:

Question from a parent:

I don't like my teenager's new friends—what can I do?

This is a very common issue as your child moves into and through their teenage years. One day they come home talking about one or two new friends. As a parent you start to notice changes in how your teenager acts, the way they talk to you, and the way they treat other people, especially their siblings. Then one day you get to meet these new friends face to face and all of your suspicions are confirmed. These new friends are a bad influence. They are the reason your once polite, respectful, conscientious teenager is acting the way they are. But what do you do?

This circumstance is a great illustration of the choice between trying to control what your teenager does versus empowering them to make the "better" choice on their own. Control involves forbidding them from being with these new friends or restricting what they can do and when they can do it. This approach has little chance of working and in fact may drive your teenager to attach even more to these new friends, just to prove their power over your attempts to control them. The alternative is to take the love-based approach of empowerment. Here are two strategies to explore.

First, engage your teenager from a place of compassion and concern over how they are doing. Note the changes you have noticed and ask if they are okay. The intention is to connect with them, increase their self-awareness, and let them discover for themselves what may be causing the changes. Here is what this might sound like:

Parent: John, it seems like you have been a little down lately. You just don't seem yourself. You and your brother have been at each other a lot more than usual. Is there something going on at school? Are you feeling stressed about your classes?

John: No, everything is fine at school.

Parent: Is there anything that is bothering you here at home?

John: No, I'm fine.

Parent: You know I just want to make sure you are doing okay. The new experiences in high school can be super exciting, but they also can be a little overwhelming. Is there anything going on with your friends? Did someone say something or do something that made you feel uncomfortable?

John: I am fine. Can you just drop it?

Parent: Yeah. Okay. But something certainly seems different with you. If you come up with anything, I would love to hear about it.

With this approach, you have strengthened your connection, you have acknowledged a change in their behavior, and you have respected their judgment while at the same time challenging them to solve a problem.

Second, continue to develop the environment within your home. Your home is a reference point for your teenager. If it is full of peace, joy, warmth, and love they will be able to recognize the difference in a "bad" friendship or relationship. Many times they will not be able to express what is going on, but it will just not feel right. When a new friend is unloving toward them or anyone else, they will feel uncomfortable.

The goal for you is to intentionally choose love over fear irrespective of the circumstance and then empower your teenager to do the same.

Here is a new perspective for you to consider. Maybe your teenager can be a "good" influence on the new "bad" friend. Maybe your teenager can become a source of healing and make a difference with this other person. Remember, when we choose a loving perspective, all bad behavior is seen as a call for love.

Keep in mind that it may take days, weeks, or even months for your teenager to process what is going on in these new friendships. While you may see the circumstance clearly, don't lose sight of the learning opportunity these circumstances provide for your teenager. They will learn through these experiences. Your role is to provide a loving environment and empower them to be their absolute best.

Making bad choices on Saturday night:

Question from a parent:

How can I help my teen make good choices when they are out with other teens?

This may be the biggest question that we face as parents of a teenager. Our fears make sense because the stakes are so much higher at this age than they were when our children were younger. The big four concerns are reckless driving, drugs, alcohol, and sex. Other than those, there is not much to worry about…right? The bottom line is your teenager will make choices about these things while you are not around to guide them. Consequently, our role as parents is to build a foundation of principles, values, and beliefs within our teenagers that will guide them in these moments of truth. That being said, when you say "Make good choices" as they head out the door on Saturday night, you are putting the finishing touches on the long process of empowering your teenager to be their absolute best.

Here are three keys to them actually "making good choices":

First, we must acknowledge that one of the key ways we shape our teenagers' principles, values, and beliefs is by the example we set. They are always watching us. They will take on your principles, values, and beliefs, both good and bad. What this looks like in life is this: If you and your family (including your teenager) go to a friend's house for a cookout and you have a few drinks, then you say, "I only had two drinks, so I am okay to drive," whether intentional or not you are teaching your teenager that it is okay to drink and drive. On the other hand, remember the hero's two journeys. Parenting is a personal development program for you as well. This is an awesome opportunity for you and ultimately a gift to your teenager. As your teenager watches you working toward being your absolute best, they will be inspired to do the same and with this will come a strong sense of self. It is this strong sense of self that will be with them on Saturday night helping to guide their choices. Never underestimate the impact of the example you set.

Second, they need a north star. A point of reference. I have said this at other times in the book, but if they know what it feels like to be in a loving environment they will be able to recognize when they are in an unloving environment. The north star is your home. When their friends are teasing them or trying to get them to drink or take drugs, they will be drawn back to the peace, joy, warmth, and love within your home. Or when they are being pushed into having sex by friends or the person they're dating and the million other outside influences, they will have a point of reference. They will have a basis for comparing what they are feeling. Even if they cannot verbalize what they experienced, they will know that it doesn't feel "right" and be more attracted to making a good decision. For example: You teenage son will show up at home two hours before you expected him. When you ask why he is home early, he will say, "I just felt like coming home." In reality, one of his friends was planning to use a fake ID to buy some beer and they were going to have a car party. He will not be able to put into words what he was feeling. He just felt something that made him feel uncomfortable. And it felt uncomfortable because he had a north star. A home that is full of peace, joy, warmth, and love can be very powerful in the life of a teenager. While you can't completely eliminate the possibility of your teenager making bad choices, this "north star" will provide a guiding light.

Finally, all of those times when you choose empowerment over control will serve them well on Saturday night. Through your commitment to empowerment you have taught your teenager to make decisions, to trust their abilities, and to understand that they are responsible for the consequences of their decisions and mistakes. They have been learning to be thoughtful and have developed a strong self image. This sounds like a teenager who you can send out on a Saturday night with confidence, doesn't it?

When to say no vs. when to say yes:

Most of the circumstances we have explored so far have been related to unwanted or negative behavior. In this case, let's look at how to approach opportunities presented to your teenager.

Here is an example: I was speaking with a father about how his teenage daughter was doing and he proudly said she was doing great. She was fully engaged at her high school. Her grades were very good and she had a good group of friends. Then his face shifted from pride to concern as he said, "We are dealing with one challenge...but it is a good challenge." He went on to explain that his daughter had been chosen to participate in a study abroad program in France during her senior year. This was an honor and super exciting for his daughter, but he had concerns about her being gone for that long, let alone being that far from home. The deadline for making a decision was quickly approaching, and he and his wife were torn on what to do.

In situations like this, you should expect your teenager to offer many arguments in favor of the new adventure. Even if, underneath, they are feeling anxious or a little afraid, most will not admit this, especially to their parents, the people who hold the power to make this decision.

So what do you do? How do you know what is the right decision for your son or daughter?

There is actually no right or wrong decision in a situation like this. Every child is different and every family circumstance is different. This is a time when a parent has to tune in to and trust their intuition. This can best be accomplished by intentionally working to deepen your connection with your teenager.

The quality of the connection will provide two benefits. First, through a strong connection, you will gain valuable insight into the readiness of your teenager to take on whatever the adventure is. Are they mature enough? Do they have the ability to make good decisions if they get in a tough spot? Are they really afraid to go and hoping you won't say yes? These insights will also provide you comfort in the middle of the night if you say yes. Second, if the ultimate decision is to say no, your teenager will know that you seriously considered their point of view and they will be able to share their disappointment without fear of retribution.

So how can you use this decision-making process as a way to build connection? The two connection-building skills that fit the best here are being present and being curious. When you discuss these options with your teenager, be very intentional about staying present. Pay attention to your emotions and feelings as the conversation progresses. If you start to experience any fear-based feelings, pause and bring your attention back to your teenager. It may be helpful to intentionally look for opportunities to acknowledge and validate what they are saying. If you can stay present, you will be able to recognize opportunities to ask questions from a place of curiosity.

What do you mean when you say...?
What would it feel like to be that far away from home?
What excites you most?
What are you most afraid of?

This approach will provide valuable information for your intuition to process as well as communicating to your teenager that you honor who they are and that you want what is best for them.

In the end, you will have to make a decision. These opportunities and subsequent decisions, whether it is a yes or a no, are tremendous growth opportunities for you and your teenager. They are milestones along your journeys.

Bonus thought: There is a difference between the "*never* no" and the "*not now* no." In many of these situations the "no" is really a "not now." As your teenager continues to grow and mature, there will be new opportunities to consider.

"How do I get my teenager to talk to me?"

This question comes up all the time. Parents come to me completely frustrated with the one-word answers they get from their teenagers.

Parent: How did you do on the math test today?

Teenager: Fine.

Parent: Are you scheduled to work this weekend?

Teenager: Yeah.

Parent: What time is Tommy picking you up tonight?

Teenager: 6:30.

We have all been there.

When we make building a connection a priority rather than just gathering information, you will notice the questions you are asking may be the issue. Many times, the questions we are asking are results oriented. They are focused on finding out what happened or what is going to happen. From your teenager's perspective, the answers to these questions open them up to possible criticism or judgment. In order to protect themselves, they answer with as little information as possible or are as vague as possible.

The solution is to shift your focus from results to process. Ask questions that challenge them to think and share their perspective.

Here are some examples:

Parent: How did you feel when you read the first question on your math test today?

Parent: When someone complains at work, how do you deal with it?

Parent: You and Tommy have been best friends since third grade. What do you think makes your friendship work so well?

One of the strategies for building connections is being curious. Challenge yourself to be curious about what your teenager is thinking and feeling, not just what they are doing. You may be surprised by how thoughtful they can be.

Note: When you ask these kinds of questions, your teenager may not have a ready answer. Be careful not to push too hard for an answer right away. Do not be surprised if they bring the conversation back up after they have processed the question for a couple of days.

The number one thing your teenager wishes you would do better:

What do you think that thing might be? In his book *Staying Connected to Your Teenager*, Michael Riera states that the most important thing is to listen. Through my experience as a family enrichment coach, I would have to agree. The interesting paradox is this. One of the most common frustrations I hear from parents is that their teenager won't talk to them. Parents are searching for strategies to get their sons or daughters to open up. The answer is really quite obvious. If you want you teenager to talk more, work on being a better listener.

The challenge parents face when listening to their teenager is the urge to control or fix whatever is going on.

Think about the last time your teenager shared a problem or issue with you. Did you shift into lecture mode? Did you get mad at them for not using better judgment? Did you offer advice or tell them what to do? My question for you is: What were you feeling as your teenager was sharing their problem? Experience tells me that your answer will be something along the lines of frustration, disappointment, or, the big one: worry.. We want our children to be safe and happy. Consequently, it is hard to see them struggling. But remember, these emotions are the indicators of fear-based principles values and beliefs. They provide a window into your mindset at that moment. Any response from a fearful perspective will only serve to make the situation worse. Think of it this way: Your teenager is already experiencing fear or doubt, otherwise there wouldn't be a problem. If your response is fear based, you are validating their fear, which will do little to move them forward.

The alternative is to see these struggles as an opportunity to connect with and empower your teenager. From this perspective, instead of experiencing frustration, disappointment, and worry, you will feel compassion and forgiveness while at the same time being grateful for the opportunity for growth the circumstance presents for your teenager. Remember, these emotions are indicators of love-based principles, values, and beliefs. Instead of lecturing or telling them what to do, you will naturally acknowledge and validate what they are going through. Your presence will comfort them and make them feel safe, while at the same time communicate to them that they are loved unconditionally and that you believe in their ability to solve their own problems.

Choosing fear-based actions will always be destructive. They will damage your connection and disempower your son or daughter.

Choosing love-based actions will always heal. They will strengthen your connection and empower your son or daughter.

The challenge for you as a parent is to continue to develop your ability to recognize the difference between the two mindsets and then exercising your power to choose between the two.

I would assert that when your teenager says that they want you to be a better listener, they are really asking you to be a love-based listener.

Big talks—Drugs, alcohol, sex:

Here is an idea for you. Instead of having big talks about these high-stakes topics, have many little conversations. Here are the two extreme scenarios for how a "big talk" typically happens.

Scenario #1

You will plan for weeks or even months to have a big talk. Then you wait for the perfect opportunity to bring up the subject, but the right time just never presents itself. After a few weeks of feeling guilty for not following through, you finally say to your teenager, "I have something we need to talk about. How about we take a walk after dinner?" In effect, you make an appointment to have the talk. The time comes and you strategically make your way through the talking points you have laid out. Your teenager acts like they are listening, but they are clearly uncomfortable.

As you wrap up your comments, you ask if they have any questions. In typical teenager fashion, they say, "No, I'm good." At this point you feel a huge sense of relief, knowing that you have fulfilled your obligation as a parent.

Scenario #2

You and your teenage son or daughter are out getting gas for the car and another teenager pulls up to the pump next to you. It is impossible not to notice because they have the sound system in their car at full volume. The song that is playing as they pull up is clearly advocating for drinking and having sex. As you get back into the car you say, "I certainly hope you don't listen to that kind of music." Your teenager responds, "It is just a song...no big deal." The phrase "no big deal" officially pushes your buttons and you launch into the big talk. Your teenager sits quietly as you lecture about being responsible and the potential consequences of making bad decisions. As you pull back into the driveway, you are satisfied that your son or daughter now knows where you stand on these big topics.

There are many other scenarios I could use to illustrate the same point. It is very common for these talks to play out with the parent doing all of the talking and the teenager not really listening. Also, since these are difficult topics, once we have the big talk, it gets marked off the list and never comes up again. In our minds, we have said our piece and there is no need to overdo it.

While there can be some value in these one-way conversations, there is another approach. I recommend that instead of thinking in terms of the "big talk," consider the possibility of having an ongoing conversation that will last throughout your son or daughter's teenage years. In these smaller conversations, allow your teenager to do most of the talking. You may be thinking, "Sounds awesome, but how do I do that?" The answer involves a combination of awareness of opportunities to bring up these big topics and our strategies for connecting and empowerment coaching. Here is a scenario to consider:

Let's use the example involving the trip to get gas for the car. The song lyrics present an opportunity to explore your teenager's current mindset regarding drinking alcohol and having sex. Here is what this conversation could sound like:

Parent: (with a smile and a hint of sarcasm) Boy, that was some really pleasant music.

Teenager: The louder the better.

Parent: Did I hear it right? It sounded like they were talking about getting girls drunk and then having sex with them.

Teenager: Yeah, but it is just a song and it has a great beat.

Parent: Great beat aside, how would you feel if one of your friends told you that they got a girl drunk and then had sex with her? Would you be okay with that?

From here, let them talk. Be grateful for the opportunity to have this conversation. Be compassionate and forgiving if you hear anything that is difficult to hear. Continue to ask questions grounded in curiosity.

At some point in the conversation, you may feel the desire to share your principles, values, and beliefs on the topic. There are two prerequisites that will greatly increase the possibility that your teenager will actually hear and consider what you are saying. The first prerequisite has been met already. You have demonstrated that you honor your teenager's thoughts and opinions by the way you have listened and asked questions. In short, they feel that they have been heard. The second prerequisite is to ask permission. Here is what that could sound like:

Parent: I am impressed by how thoughtful you are being right now. You have made a few points that I have not considered before. Would it be okay if I shared a few of my thoughts with you?

When they say yes, it is your turn to express your perspective. After you state your case, check in with them again as a way to continue the conversation. Try this:

Parent: Does what I am saying make sense to you? What do you agree with and what do you disagree with?

Continue the conversation until it feels like it has run its course or until there is a natural transition, like you pull back into the driveway or someone walks into the room. Wrap up the conversation with gratitude and set the stage for future discussion. You could say:

Parent: I really appreciate you being this open with me, as well as your willingness to hear me out. If you ever feel like you need to talk more, I am here.

This approach feels doable, doesn't it?

So where does it go from here? Continue to look for natural opportunities to bring up these big topics. Here are a few examples:

- You are watching a movie and the plot involves someone getting hit by a drunk driver.
- You overhear your teenager talking about a girl at school who is pregnant.

- Your teen brings home a pamphlet from school on safe sex.
- You see a group of teens standing outside the local Dairy Queen smoking cigarettes or vaping.
- You see an ad on TV that makes drinking look glamorous. You could ask your teenager if they knew that there used to be ads for cigarettes on TV but they are not allowed now. Follow up with: Should ads for alcohol be allowed?

When you start looking, these opportunities are everywhere.

Here is an idea that one parent came up with:

Parent: I have a question. What are you going to say when one of your friends gets in the car with a 12-pack of beer?

Teenager: What are you talking about? That is not going to happen.

Parent: Maybe not, but it could. I would feel a lot better if I knew you had thought about and practiced what you would say if it did happen. What would you say?

Teenager: I would tell them that I just got my license and I don't want to lose it by drinking and driving. Put the beer in the trunk and you guys can do whatever you want with it later.

Parent: I can picture you saying that. If I start to get worried about you tonight I am going to imagine you being self-confident and saying that. That makes me feel better.

This conversation does two things. First, having that image in your mind and being able to hear your teenager doing the right thing will be comforting at 11:15 when you start to have the inevitable fear-based thoughts. Secondly, research has shown that when your teenager practices and actually says out loud what they would say in one of the tough situations, they are much more likely to be able to do it in the heat of the moment.

One final note on these conversations: Continue to present the possible consequences in a way that shifts the responsibility for these consequences to your teenager. For example you could ask: What would you do for money if you got kicked out of high school for drinking and couldn't go to college?

Keep this in mind: When your teenager is faced with making a decision involving one of these big topics, you will not be there. This is why your commitment to empowering them to be their absolute best is so important.

Disrupting the family:

Question from a parent:

How can I get my teenager to create less disruption in our family?

The natural follow up is: What do you mean by being disruptive?

There are many variations, but here are a few examples of the issues I hear:

- My son is always picking fights with his younger brother.
- Every time we go out to dinner as a family, my daughter never looks up from her phone and when we bring it up she gets upset and ruins the evening for the whole family.

- Sometimes my teenage son takes forever to get dressed after his football practice. He knows that we take his sister to her piano lesson after we pick him up. Three times this month he was so slow that she missed her lesson completely. There are times when I think he is doing this on purpose.
- Our house has become the go-to place for my daughter and her friends. At first I liked the idea of them being at our house, but as time has gone on it has become a problem. Their music keeps getting louder. They leave behind a mess everywhere they go in the house and last week they knocked over a book shelf and broke several picture frames.

For this topic, I feel like the first step is to revisit a few of the fundamental elements of a love-based mindset.

First, we recognize that before we can have any hope of influencing or empowering our teenager to make better decisions about their behavior, we have to build a strong connection.

Second, from a loving perspective, we see this unwanted or "bad" behavior as a call for love. A call to reconnect.

These two insights obviously will lead us to implementing the strategies for building connection, but there is another fundamental element we need to consider.

In order to effectively build connection with your teenager, the parent has to be firmly grounded in a love-based mindset. This requires intentionally choosing love over fear in the heat of the moment.

Consider this. Whatever the issue, if you are viewing it from a fearful mindset you will see one set of potential solutions. However, if you are viewing the circumstance from a loving mindset, you will see a completely different set of potential solutions. Ultimately, the actions you take will come from the options you see. I say all of this to point out the impact your thought system has on the action you take and the corresponding results.

So back to the disruptive teenager. I would assert that, just like you, your teenager has both a fear-based thought system and a love-based thought system. In these moments when they are being disruptive, they are acting from a fear-based perspective. They do not intend to be disruptive, but they find themselves in a particular circumstance that stirs up fear and they respond. They are afraid of what their friends will think and say about them. They are afraid that they won't fit in or that they aren't good enough. And, as we have discussed, any response from a fearful perspective will be destructive.

When you are facing a disruptive circumstance, follow these steps:

1. Resist being drawn into a negative, fear-based mindset.
2. Ask yourself what are the natural consequences your teen should be responsible for as the result of their disruptive behavior? For example: When your daughter and her friends break a bookshelf, she should be responsible for paying for a replacement.
3. With compassion and an intention to empower, communicate that the teen will be responsible for natural consequences. If needed, explain how your teen's actions/decision led to the consequence.
4. Resist the urge to rescue them when they complain.

Breaking curfew:

Curfew is typically not an issue until your teenager starts driving, although it can come into play when they go places with friends or boyfriends/girlfriends who are driving. The driver's license provides the freedom to make the decision on when to come home, and in your teenager's mind, shifts the responsibility for making this decision from you to them. The first step in dealing with issues around curfews is to do a serious assessment of your state of mind on the topic. What is the problem a curfew solves? I ask this because it is possible for this topic to be a tremendous opportunity to build connection with your teenager rather than becoming an ongoing source of conflict.

You are probably thinking, "How can that be?"

First, clearly identify the problem the curfew solves for you. For most parents, it is about the safety of their child and their own peace of mind. There is nothing worse than the feeling in the pit of your gut when your teenager is 30 minutes late getting home on a Saturday night and you haven't heard from them. Additionally, we have this belief that nothing good happens after midnight...right?

The next step in turning this potential conflict into a source of connection is to share the problem with your teenager and ask them to help come up with a solution that works for both of you. You could say something like this:

Parent: Now that you have your driver's license, I know that you are going to want to go out with your friends and do things on the weekends. While this is exciting for you, it presents a couple of problems for me as a parent.

135

First of all, I have a responsibility to help you stay out of circumstances or environments that you feel like you are not ready for yet. This is a balancing act between my sense of your experience, maturity, and ability to make good choices and your desire to be out doing what teenagers do on a Friday or Saturday night. I want this to work for both of us, but you should know that I am feeling a little hesitant. In order for me to feel like I am being responsible as a parent, I would like to set up some agreements for how we are going to communicate about where you are and what you are doing, as well as what time you are going to be home. What ideas do you have about this?

Can you see how this invites your teenager to join you in the process of managing future Friday and Saturday nights?

Can you see the difference between these two mindsets for your teenager at 10:45 on a Friday night?

Teenager: *My mom told me* I have to be home by 11:00. This curfew is so random and dumb.

Vs.

Teenager: *I told my mom* that I would be home at 11:00 so I'd better get going.

Please note that I am not suggesting that you just agree to whatever your teenager proposes. Clearly state that this solution has to work for both you and them. Hear them out and then present your concerns and ideas. If you find yourself miles apart, introduce the idea of your teenager building trust over a period of time. Set some conditions

136

for communication and times to be home. Then agree to revisit the conversation at a designated time. (Part of your trust building is to honor this agreement to reopen the conversation at the designated time.) Allow them the opportunity to "earn" your trust and demonstrate the maturity and ability to make good decisions.

Remember: A change in perspective changes everything.

This is as true for "curfew" as it is for any of the other issues you face with your teenager.

The power of a handwritten note:

One of the most under-appreciated ways to build connection and empower your teenager is to handwrite a note. This can be done as a way to heal your relationship after an argument or as a way to communicate how much you love and believe in them. Here is what you do: After an unusually difficult week of fighting over everything from how clean their room is to getting their homework done to not calling when they were going to be late getting home, you write something like this and put it somewhere they will see it:

John,

I know this last week has been tough for us. I am sorry for yelling at you, but when I get frustrated it is hard for me to stop. I know that it never really helps and going forward I am going to try to be more understanding.

More importantly, I want you to know that even though we disagree and fight sometimes, I still love you. You are my son and I will always love you no matter what.

Have a great day at school.

I love you,

Dad

Now, don't expect your son or daughter to immediately acknowledge your note. In fact, they may never bring it up, but be assured that they read it. In fact, I know of a case in which one young man said that he kept all of the notes his parents had written him during high school. He shared that these notes helped him get through his freshman year at college. He loved reading them whenever he was feeling homesick or down about something.

- How about a note of encouragement on the day of a big test?
- How about a note of appreciation if they help a younger sibling with their homework?

You get the idea: Grab a pen and start writing.

Conflict—Crossing your teen's will:

Your teenager will continue to stretch the limits and challenge you to see the world through their eyes. When you think about it, this makes sense. They are going through the process of becoming independent. Of becoming their own person. These conflicts come out of the distance between how they see themselves and how we see them as their parents. With a strong-willed teenager, this can lead to slammed doors, disgusted looks, or harsh words. I am sure some of you can relate to this.

As always, the solution lies in shifting from control to empowerment—from a fear-based mindset to a love-based mindset. Let's review the three key steps for making this transformation.

Step one:

Take some time to reflect on what is going on for you, the parent. It is time for some self-awareness to assess your mindset.

- What feelings are coming up for you?
- What are you most afraid of?
- What are the core beliefs that are driving your fears?
- How else could you look at the circumstance?

Again, the goal during this time of reflection is to determine if your perspective is fear based or love based. If you find that it is fear based, use the techniques we have discussed earlier to intentionally reconnect with love-based principles, values, and beliefs. This can't be emphasized enough: In order to transform your relationship with your teenager and the environment within your home, you will need to be very **intentional** about what is going on inside of you. Identify ahead of time what triggers you need to be aware of and what feelings signal that you are being pulled into a fearful mindset. Use this awareness the next time things get heated. Ask for a pause. Acknowledge what is going on for you. You absolutely have the power to choose between a love- or fear-based thought system. The question is, will you exercise this power?

Step two:

Once you are grounded in love, turn your attention to building connections. Which the strategies for building connection do you see working best given your circumstance and the current state of the relationship with your teenager? Again, be intentional. For example: As you are waiting for your teenager to get into the car, close your eyes and state your intention for how you want the ten minutes you will have in the car on the way home to go. Say it out loud. This could sound something like this:

My intention is to stay grounded in love during the next ten minutes with Bobby. If I notice myself becoming frustrated, I will return to compassion and forgiveness. Even if we don't say anything, my goal is to communicate through my presence my unconditional love for my son. Curiosity about what he is thinking will work best for building connections. I will be present and listen with an open mind.

Saying this aloud may feel a little weird at first, but would it still seem weird if you had a great ride home and actually felt a deepening connection?

Step three:

In steps one and two, you intentionally chose love and worked to deepen your connection. Now it is time to move from conflict with your strong-willed teenager to empowerment.

With a fresh set of eyes, look at the issues that are causing the most conflict between you and your teenager. What is your son or daughter trying to communicate to you? This would be a great time to acknowledge the conflict, state your intention to be a source of empowerment, and ask them to share their perspective. Try something like this:

Bobby, these last few months have been tough for us. It feels like every time we talk it turns into an argument. It won't be long and you are going to be out on your own. I am excited for you (and I know you are excited too), but there are other times when I feel a combination of sadness and worry. I have noticed that our fights always happen when I am feeling worried and try to control things too much. I want you to know that I am sorry about that. If you knew I wouldn't get mad and it wouldn't turn into a fight, what would you like to say to me?

Whatever comes out of their mouth at this point should be heard with compassion and forgiveness. Stay grounded in love because love always heals. Then shift to empowerment. Put into practice the coaching skills discussed earlier. Seek clarity, then acknowledge and validate what is going on for them. Encourage them to cast a vision of where they want to be and how they see themselves in the future—six months, one year, five years. Help them identify and break through any limiting beliefs that are holding them back. Support them in developing an action plan for moving forward. Ask what they can do today to get some movement forward and momentum. And don't forget to celebrate their successes and be a source of inspiration.

These conversations can be very powerful for both you and your teenager. You will gain insight into your teenager and your teenager will gain insight into you. Best of all, experience tells me that most of the big conflicts will just magically go away as you make the shift from control to empowerment.

If you are willing to listen, your teenager will provide valuable feedback for your growth as a parent.

Over my 35 years as a parent, I have sought advice and counsel from friends, relatives, courses, and books. I have also discovered that if you are open to it, sometimes the best feedback on how to be a parent will come from your own children. This is another one of the advantages of a love-based mindset. When I am grounded in love, I am open to receive wisdom from any and all sources. But when I am grounded in fear, I am too busy defending myself and making excuses to recognize the lesson right in front of me.

Here is a story from my first book, *Because I Said So*, that illustrates this point.

I am writing this in response to a disturbing trend in youth athletics: the growing number of incidents between parents, coaches, and referees during youth athletic events. If you have spent any time around a soccer field, basketball court, or baseball/softball diamond, you have probably witnessed parents or coaches displaying questionable judgment. As a parent of six children ages two to eighteen, I have coached or watched everything from four-year-old kids playing three-on-three soccer to a Level 1 AAU 12-and-under national basketball tournament to high school varsity football.

During the thousands of games I have watched or coached, I have seen gestures of true sportsmanship and decency that would warm any person's heart: Two players helping each other up off the floor. A fan/parent seeking out a player on the opposing team to offer sincere congratulations for a game well-played and good sportsmanship.

However, I have also seen unexplainable acts of anger and abuse: A grandparent physically pushing a coach, causing an entire team of six-year-old soccer players to start crying. A father bordering on verbal abuse with a ten-year-old basketball player for mistakes made on the floor. A mother encouraging her child to intentionally injure players from the opposing team. All in the name of sport.

As a fan or coach, it is easy to get caught up in the emotion of a game, but we have to make sure we don't forget that we are parents first. I would like to pass along the best piece of advice I have ever heard on parenting a young athlete. This piece of wisdom came from my 13-year-old daughter, Brittany. We were driving to a soccer game, and for some reason, I felt compelled to review the game plan. I was rambling on about playing hard on defense and pushing the ball wide on offense, when I noticed that she didn't appear to be listening. I have to admit, I was a little concerned about her lack of interest in my vast soccer knowledge, but she seemed genuinely upset. So I asked her what was wrong.

She looked up at me and said, "Why can't you just be my dad?" I thought to myself that this was a reasonable request, but I have to admit that it caught me off guard. What does it mean to just be a mom or dad to a young athlete?

- It means that you are the first one to forgive a missed shot, a dropped ball, or a bad call by the referee.
- It means that you will offer love and support, regardless of the outcome of the game.
- It means that you measure success in terms of participation, effort, and fair play.
- It means that you promote having fun as the number one objective.
- It means that you understand that the game is just a game.
- It means that you are a fan of the team, and the parent of a child.

Sometimes, the obvious can only be seen when we look from another perspective. If you want to do what is right for your young athlete, take the advice of a 13-year-old girl: Don't ever forget that your first job is to be a parent.

Empowering your teenager to overcome mean-spirited comments:

Question from a parent:

What do I do when my daughter comes home upset because other kids are saying mean things to her?

Unfortunately, meanness is a growing issue within our schools and on social media. With daughters, these comments are often directed at appearance. One girl tells another that she is ugly or her hair looks stupid. To a 15-year-old, comments like this can be devastating. Especially if they come from someone who is considered a friend or someone who has influence within the school community.

I would like to offer two strategies for empowering your teenager to overcome these mean-spirited comments.

Before we explore these strategies, let's drill down on the root cause of the pain or upset for a teenager who is on the receiving end of a mean comment. At the core, these comments stir up the fear of not being good enough, not belonging, and not being worthy of love. We all can agree these are three of the big ones. Interestingly, these three fears continue to follow all of us into our adult years as well. For example: Instead of in response to a mean comment about how our hair looks today, these fears come up when a co-worker disagrees with a decision we made or a boss expresses concern about our job performance. So, one of

144

the greatest gifts you can give to your teenager is a strong sense of connection and a love-based self-image. Not only will these attributes help today with the mean-spirited comment, they will serve them well for the rest of their life.

The first strategy I am going to suggest is intended to build your connection with your teenager. A strong connection with you and your home will help to lessen the intensity of the fear your daughter experiences when one of these mean-spirited comments comes her way. In reality there is no way to completely eliminate her upset, but a strong connection can certainly reduce it. I like to think of it as a continuum. A teenage girl who feels no sense of connection to her parents or her home will experience the fear of not belonging at a level 10, while the girl who has a strong connection will be at a 2 or 3. Your goal is to continually build connection so that your teenager is less and less vulnerable over time.

In Part 3, we explored nine ways to build the connection between a parent and their teenager. For this topic, it seemed appropriate to revisit "Acts of Kindness." This strategy, based on Gary Chapman's *5 Love Languages*, is great for giving your teenager a sense that not only are they loved but, even more importantly, they are worthy of love. As a reminder, the five love languages are:

- Words of affirmation
- Acts of service
- Quality time
- Receiving gifts
- Physical touch

Which one of these does your teenager seem to crave the most? Your goal is to be intentional about engaging with your teenager in their particular love language on a regular basis. Doing this will move your daughter down the scale of vulnerability.

The second strategy involves empowering your teenager in this case to have a love-based mindset. This could be accomplished by sharing one of the fundamental principles discussed in Part 3. All "bad" or "unwanted" behavior is a call for love.

You could say:

I wonder what is going on for her that makes her feel like she has to be mean?

Can you see how this question introduces the idea of compassion into your teenager's mind? It is not that this other teenager is a bad person, it is that they are struggling with something. As your teenager develops the ability to see the world from a loving perspective, they will begin to see the "mean" comments as a cry for help rather than an attack.

Here is something to consider: What if through your efforts to build connection and empower your teenager to engage with others from a love-based mindset, your teenager became a positive influence in the "mean" girl's life. That would be a gift to everyone.

Why your teenager needs to make mistakes:

One of the traps of parenting a teenager is the urge we feel to share our wisdom. We see our son or daughter heading down a path that we know from our own experience is not going anywhere good. So, we sit them down and tell them how we have been there before. How they need to listen to our advice so that they don't make the same mistakes we did. In our minds this makes perfect sense—we are just trying to steer our teenager away from potential pain and suffering.

The problem is nine times out of ten, they won't take your good advice; in fact, sometimes it feels like they do the opposite just to prove you wrong.

My recommendation is that you embrace the power of experiential learning and focus your attention on empowering them to solve their own problems.

In simple terms, experiential learning is learning by doing. The premise is that it is only through personal experience that we can truly "get" something. I like to think of it as knowing about a topic vs. really understanding how to do something. For example: You can know all about how to ride a bike, but the only way to really learn to ride a bike is to get on it and start pedaling. And we do this with the knowledge that we are going to have to fall a few times before we eventually "get" it.

In the same way, your teenager can know all about good study habits, but the only way for them to "get" what works is for them to try and fail a few times. Or while you can share all of the reasons why their new boyfriend or girlfriend is not good for them, the lessons they will learn from the experience of figuring out they are not happy in the relationship and eventually breaking up with the person will serve them for the rest of their life.

Here is a perspective shift for you to consider:

Rather than helping your teenager avoid a potential mistake today, put your attention on teaching them to be resourceful so they can overcome today's mistake.

Resourcefulness is a skill they will use today, tomorrow, and every day of their lives.

Bonus: The Teddy Stoddard Story

As I was approaching the end of this book, this story popped up for me—and even though it isn't about parenting a teenager, it does illustrate everything this book is trying to communicate. How a shift in perspective changes everything. The healing power of love. How building connection and empowerment can be transformative. Also, look for the hero's two journeys. Both for Mrs. Thompson and Teddy. This story was originally published *HomeLife* magazine and was written by Elizabeth Silance Ballard.

–(Call me a softy, but I can't read this story without tearing up at the end. You may want to have some tissues handy.)

Many years ago, there was an elementary teacher named Mrs. Thompson. And as she stood in front of her fifth-grade class on the first day of school, she told the children a lie. Like most teachers, she looked at her students and said that she loved them all the same. But that was impossible, because there in the front row, slumped in his seat, was a little boy named Teddy Stoddard.

Mrs. Thompson had watched Teddy the year before and noticed that he didn't play well with the other children, that his clothes were messy, and that he constantly needed a bath. And Teddy could be unpleasant.

It got to the point where Mrs. Thompson would actually take delight in marking his papers with a broad red pen, making bold X's and then putting a big F at the top.

At the school where Mrs. Thompson taught, she was required to review each child's past records and she put Teddy's off until last.

However, when she reviewed his file, she was in for a surprise.

Teddy's first-grade teacher wrote, "Teddy is a bright child with a ready laugh. He does his work neatly and has good manners...he is a joy to be around."

His second-grade teacher wrote, "Teddy is an excellent student, well-liked by his classmates, but he is troubled because his mother has a terminal illness and life at home must be a struggle."

His third-grade teacher wrote, "His mother's death has been hard on him. He tries to do his best, but his father doesn't show much interest and his home life will soon affect him if some steps aren't taken."

Teddy's fourth-grade teacher wrote, "Teddy is withdrawn and doesn't show much interest in school. He doesn't have many friends and sometimes sleeps in class."

By now, Mrs. Thompson realized the problem and she was ashamed of herself. She felt even worse when her students brought her Christmas presents—all wrapped in beautiful ribbons and bright paper, except for Teddy's.

His present was clumsily wrapped in the heavy, brown paper that he got from a grocery bag. Mrs. Thompson took pains to open it in the middle of the other presents. Some of the children started to laugh when she found a rhinestone bracelet with some of the stones missing and a bottle that was one-quarter full of perfume.

But she stifled the children's laughter when she exclaimed how pretty the bracelet was, putting it on, and dabbing some of the perfume on her wrist.

Teddy Stoddard stayed after school that day just long enough to say, "Mrs. Thompson, today you smelled just like my Mom used to."

After the children left, she cried for at least an hour. On that very day, she quit teaching reading, and writing, and arithmetic. Instead, she began to teach children. Mrs. Thompson paid particular attention to Teddy.

As she worked with him, his mind seemed to come alive The more she encouraged him, the faster he responded. By the end of the year, Teddy had become one of the smartest children in the class and, despite her lie that she would love all the children the same, Teddy became one of her "teacher's pets."

A year later, she found a note under her door from Teddy, telling her that she was still the best teacher he ever had in his whole life.

Six years went by before she got another note from Teddy. He then wrote that he had finished high school, third in his class, and she was still the best teacher he ever had in his whole life.

Four years after that, she got another letter, saying that while things had been tough at times, he'd stayed in school and would soon graduate from college with the highest of honors. He assured Mrs. Thompson that she was still the best teacher he ever had in his whole life.

Then four more years passed and yet another letter came.

This time he explained that after he got his bachelor's degree, he decided to go a little further. The letter explained that she was still his favorite teacher. But now his name was a little longer. The letter was signed, Theodore F. Stoddard, M.D.

The story doesn't end there. You see, there was yet another letter that spring. Teddy said he'd met this woman and was going to be married. He explained that his father had died a couple of years before and he was wondering if Mrs. Thompson might agree to sit in the place at the wedding that was usually reserved for the mother of the groom.

Of course, Mrs. Thompson did. And guess what? She wore that bracelet, the one with several rhinestones missing. And she made sure she was wearing the perfume that Teddy remembered his mother wearing.

They hugged each other, and Dr. Stoddard whispered in Mrs. Thompson's ear, "Thank you, Mrs. Thompson, for believing in me. Thank you so much for making me feel important and showing me that I could make a difference."

Mrs. Thompson, with tears in her eyes, whispered back. She said, "Teddy, you have it all wrong. You were the one who taught me that I could make a difference. I didn't know how to teach until I met you."

Conclusion:

My intention with this book has been to focus on the parent-child relationship, specifically the job of parenting a teenager. Interestingly, the same techniques we have been exploring to transform your relationship with your teenager can also have a major impact on all of your family relationships. Your relationship with your spouse. Your relationship with your former spouse. Your relationship with your step-children. Your relationship with your mother or father. Your relationship with your in-laws. Your relationship with your siblings. Your relationship with your friends.

So I am going to challenge you.

Be the hero in your family. Take a stand for the healing power of love.

Now, before you say that you can't do that or don't want that kind of responsibility, consider this:

The first person you can be a hero for is yourself. Remember the hero's two journeys. What if as you developed your abilities to choose love over fear, to build deep connections, and to be a source of empowerment, you transformed your *own* life? What if you found peace, joy, and a sense of purpose like you have never felt before?

THIS IS POSSIBLE.

Could it be that the struggles you are dealing with in your marriage, the difficulty of the divorce, the issues you are facing as a step parent, , your difficult relationship with your in-laws, or your concerns about your teenager are exactly what you need in order to grow at this point in your life? The biggest breakthroughs are typically born out of the most difficult times.

Remember my definition of a *successful family*?

A *successful family* is one whose members speak with respect, honor difference, provide a nurturing environment, empower each other, and truly enjoy being together.

This family has a knack for really enjoying and appreciating the good times, while at the same time, they can effectively deal with any difficult issues that come their way. There is a sense of peace, joy, warmth, and love within their home.

Why not your family? Why not today?

About the Author:

Around the time Jim White's sixth child was born, his life took an unexpected turn. It started with an invitation to join a Toastmasters group. Toastmasters' mission is to help its members improve their speaking skills. In order to focus on delivery techniques and getting over any stage fright, members are encouraged to talk about topics they are comfortable with. Being a father of six children, Jim naturally talked about dad stuff. In fact, most of his speeches were focused on the idea of teaching his children how to be "good" people or to be "successful."

Jim's interest in the idea of being a "good" or "successful" person exploded during this time. Over the next couple of years (and ever since) he found himself being drawn to books on parenting, happiness, character development, and self-improvement. Jim read continuously and began to work the ideas and concepts he was learning into his speeches at Toastmasters as well as his everyday practice of being a father.

During this time, Jim also started writing on the topic of family enrichment. Writing was a great way to process all that he was learning through reading and his attempts to apply these lessons in his own family. A few years later, Jim had accumulated enough material to put together a book. In 2004, he self-published a book titled *Because I Said So*.

It was about this time that Jim discovered the profession of life coaching and attended the iPEC coaching program. Ever since, he has been on a journey to gather as much knowledge as possible on the topics of coaching, personal development, and family enrichment.

Now, Jim finds himself at a time in his life where he is feeling called to share what he has learned over the last 40 years as a husband, a father, and now a grandfather: Papa Jim. More specifically, he is feeling called to write, speak, teach, and coach on the topic of family enrichment.

In support of this calling, Jim founded the Family Enrichment Academy to serve families and parents.

About the Family Enrichment Academy:

Vision: Our long-term vision is to heal and transform the family experience.

Mission: All of our course materials and content are designed with the mission to empower parents to choose love over fear regardless of the circumstances or how life is putting the squeeze on them.

What is the Family Enrichment Academy Support Community?

We are a growing number of parents with a common vision.

We are a community of people just like you... We are moms and dads that believe that families are meant to empower each other and that our homes are intended to be places of peace, joy, warmth, and love.

What makes us different is our commitment to choosing empowerment over control. Choosing love over fear regardless of the circumstance.

Yes...even when the circumstances of life or social pressures put the squeeze on us and try to convince us otherwise...we respond by choosing love. We do this because we know that choosing a loving perspective... changes everything.

For more information on our courses, programs, and support community, visit:

www.familyenrichmentacademy.com

"The 28-Day Parenting Boot Camp is a valuable program for parents new to the teenage years as well as for seasoned parents. We all need a little help connecting now and then, especially with our teens! Jim brings a wealth of knowledge and wisdom gained through his own experience of raising six children. Jim offers valuable advice and coaching skills to help you connect with your teenager in a loving and enriching way, and he gently guides you through the process. I highly recommend this program!"—**Pam F., parent of a 15-year-old son**

Made in the USA
Las Vegas, NV
19 February 2023

67801425R00095